W9-BKQ-033

Twayne's United States Authors Series

Sylvia E. Bowman, *Editor*

INDIANA UNIVERSITY

Richard Eberhart

Richard Eberhart

By BERNARD F. ENGEL

Michigan State University

 194

Twayne Publishers, Inc.   ::   New York

To Adele

Acknowledgments

I want to acknowledge the courtesy of Mr. and Mrs. Richard Eberhart to my wife and me, and also to thank Mr. Eberhart for the time and thought he has taken in answering letters. Mr. Joel Roache, now on the faculty at the University of Wisconsin, has generously offered more help than space limitations would allow me to use. Thanks are also due to the Baker Library at Dartmouth College, whose officers sent me copies of Mr. Eberhart's correspondence with Wallace Stevens.

Earlier versions of some passages in this study appeared in my *The Achievement of Richard Eberhart* (Scott, Foresman and Company, 1968); I thank Scott, Foresman for permission to borrow. Early versions of some passages were included in a paper, "Richard Eberhart: Something Unknown in Knowing," read at the 1968 meeting of the Midwest Modern Language Association. Some travel and secretarial expenses were covered by a Michigan State University research grant. Thanks are due to Oxford University Press for permission to quote from poems, and to Mr. Eberhart himself for permission to quote from letters to me.

Preface

IT is possible to argue that, as the astronomer should keep his gaze on his eyepiece and the baseball fan should go to the ballpark, so the reader of poetry should read poems, not books about them. But astronomers and baseball fans meet rainy days, and the poetry reader knows those times when the art itself is too demanding. Ralph Waldo Emerson got to the nub of the matter, as he often did, when he advised in "The American Scholar" that the thoughtful man should go to the source of knowledge itself, should "read God directly"; yet he also recognized that "intervals of darkness come," that there are times when the original is too rich and talk about it may revivify. There are times, too, when reading about poems can show what another reader thought of them and perhaps suggest new insight. And there is a legitimate curiosity about an author and his purposes— legitimate because works of art are produced by human beings, not by mechanical artificers.

This study begins with a brief presentation of Eberhart's views on the mission and purposes of poetry. These views ally him with the Romantics, with those who believe poetry should express inspiration and mystery. Accounts of his career, of his conversation during an interview, and of his handling of a public reading of his poems show something of the origin of his principles and something of the attitudes and practices that result from them. The study, then, considers his career in three principal stages. In the work of his early years, through publication of *Song and Idea* (1942), Eberhart first demands an almost unearthly insipiration, then accepts the need to recognize the flesh but, for the time, holds off admitting its importance. In his second stage, extending through publication of *Undercliff* (1953) and including the verse plays, Eberhart explores what he now admits is the "interinvolvement" or "interanimation" of flesh and spirit, the paradox that, with only rare exceptions, one can expect to attain intimations of the spiritual only through use of the flesh. In his third stage, beginning with publication of *Great Praises* (1957), he accepts the inability to resolve the pulls of dualism; and he praises the state of active meditation that one may achieve even while being drawn by both spirit and flesh. He becomes sure that readiness to meet destiny is the highest attainment, a readiness that is confident because he is increasingly sure that death, though it closes a final door on this life, will open a new phase of experience. The study ends with a brief look at Eberhart's reputation and suggestions for an evaluation.

BERNARD F. ENGEL

Michigan State University

Contents

Chronology

1904   Richard Eberhart born April 5 in Austin, Minnesota.
1921   Family reversals begin as his mother's fatal illness starts and his father's business suffers an embezzlement.
1922-   Study at University of Minnesota
1923
1923   Enters Dartmouth College.
1926   Bachelor of arts degree, Dartmouth College. Employment at Marshall, Field and Company, Chicago.
1927   Crosses Pacific as sailor on freighters. Eventually reaches England as a ship passenger.
1927   Enters Cambridge University. By now, is writing *A Bravery of Earth*. Harriet Monroe publishes eight of his poems in *Poetry*.
1929   Bachelor of arts degree, Cambridge. (According to British custom, Master's degree awarded in 1933 after sufficient time had elapsed and he had paid the required fee.)
1929-   Brief periods of tutoring.
1931
1930   *A Bravery of Earth*.
1931-   Study of German in Berlin.
1932
1932-   Graduate student in literature at Harvard.
1933
1933-   Master in English, Saint Mark's School, Southborough, Massa-
1941   chusetts.
1937   *Reading the Spirit*.
1941   Marriage to Elizabeth Butcher, August 29. In September, begins teaching at Cambridge School, Kendal Green, Massachusetts.
1942   *Song and Idea*.
1942-   Service as navy officer; most of the time, aerial gunnery
1946   instructor.
1945   *Poems, New and Selected*.
1946   Harriet Monroe Memorial Prize; Guarantor's Prize from *Poetry* magazine. Son Richard Butcher ("Rick") Eberhart born.
1947   *Burr Oaks*.
1946-   Full-time employment as salesman, executive, eventually vice-
1952   president, Butcher Polish Company.
1950-   Active in Poets' Theatre, Cambridge, Massachusetts; a founder
1952   and first president of the organization.

1951 Shelley Memorial Prize. *Selected Poems.*

1952 Daughter Margaret Ghormley ("Gretchen") Eberhart born.

1952- Visiting professor, poet in residence, University of Wash-
1953 ington.

1953 *Undercliff: Poems 1946-1953.*

1955 Grant from National Institute of Arts and Letters; Harriet Monroe Poetry Award.

1956 After visiting professorships at the University of Connecticut, Wheaton College (Connecticut), and Princeton, accepts appointment as professor of English and poet in residence at Dartmouth College.

1957 *Great Praises.*

1959- Consultant in Poetry, Library of Congress.
1961

1960 Elected to National Institute of Arts and Letters. *Collected Poems 1930-1960.*

1962 Bollingen Prize. *Collected Verse Plays.*

1963- Honorary Consultant in American Letters, Library of Con-
1966 gress.

1964 *The Quarry.*

1965 *Selected Poems 1930-1965.*

1966 Pulitzer Prize

1967 Phi Beta Kappa Poet, Harvard University (previous Phi Beta Kappa appointments include Tufts, 1941; Brown, 1957; Swarthmore, Trinity, and William and Mary, 1963; University of New Hampshire, 1964). *Thirty One Sonnets.*

1968 *Shifts of Being.*

1969 Named Fellow, Academy of American Poets, and given the academy's award for poetic achievement.

1970 January. Honored by Mark Sickel Symposium on Poetry, at Dartmouth. Autumn: Chatto and Windus Publishers, London, prepare selection of recent poems (as yet untitled) for publication in 1972.

1971 Joel H. Roache, *Richard Eberhart: The Progress of an American Poet.* New York: Oxford University Press.

CHAPTER 1

A Man Called to a Career

I *Affirmations of Wonder*

RICHARD Eberhart sees himself as a poet of wonder, as an artist of the mysterious who idealizes poetry as a means of expressing what he believes to be spiritual depths not accessible to the merely realistic perceiver. His prose statements on poetic art are not so direct as his poems, but there is substance even in so highflown a statement as "Why I Say It in Verse."[1] In it he says that a poet uses verse in order to give himself to "a delirium of joy, which inheres between vowels, where is the ultimate mystery of language, as being the fluid river or sea pent between rigidities or monumental masses of consonants, and is an exercise in music." He goes on to praise poetry as leading the mind "between rational essences to those other electrifying essences which blaze in the most secret hour," essences known to all men but unvoiced if not expressed by poetry.

From praise of poetry as an instrument, and as a power, for expressing the otherwise inexpressible, it is a short step to praise of it as a means to virtue. Eberhart can say that the best critics are "the arbiters of value"; for his relativism allows him to observe that they are "necessarily contained within the areas of sensibility allowed by the kind of society of which they are a product and a reflection."[2] Of verse lines that he cites as typifying "profound poetic statement," Eberhart declares: "They put you in love with life. You become identified with eternal relationships. A sweet religious essence may fill you. . . . Thus you become a part of every man; you lose your oddity. You mate with the changeless."[3]

That Eberhart's belief in the transcendent value of poetry is Emersonian does not date it, for Emerson's importance is, after all, that he gives voice to permanent elements in the bundle of variegated ideas that we consider the American tradition. Eberhart gives poetry the additional virtues of concentration and power "in the sense of insight"; and he says it should be "suggestive" rather than "finally understood"—it "should always be a mystery which may entice and satisfy the soul" that itself is always under attack by the rational mind.

The separation of mind and soul is matched in Eberhart's work by such oppositions as chaos and unity, appearance and reality, mortal and immortal. Yet Eberhart reflects that "Neither mind nor heart should dominate the being," that "Harmony and wholeness are goals of the good."[4] Eberhart's man believes himself to live in a world where what should be unified in a comprehensive harmony is divided into two or many categories and pigeonholes. Eberhart, indeed, speaks of himself as a "modern dualist," as a "relativist" who "can always see two sides, if not many, to every question."[5] The poet, he says, is "two persons, at least two." He is one who must have the energy to get along in "the world as it is, in which he does not believe," and also the energy to confront the "world of becoming, which he makes real." Eberhart also says that one must be open to the poetry that comes by "inspiration," yet be ready to make the poetry that comes by "taking thought," that has the "impurity" of the "whole warring and loving human nature of man."[6] This "dualism," this perception of a world of divisions, links Eberhart with the great Romantics;[7] and it is a central source of his drive to create poetry. He has said, indeed, that "If one were only conscious of harmony, there would be no need to write."[8]

In a world that offers him only a fragmented order, he struggles to create a personal vision that will proclaim harmony. He believes poetry to express a mysterious "essence," and he holds that, since this essence is significant for man, it is moral. His poetry is characterized by multiplicity and variety that attest to his independence from fixed creeds. Inclusive and insightful rather than narrowly systematic, it is a poetry of wonder that develops not by logical progression but by a process of maturing. In that maturing, Eberhart moves toward resolution of dualism by coming to cautious acceptance of this world as intimately involved with the world of spirit. But his accomplishment lies in his achievement of poems. We may be aware of progression in ideas without forgetting that, for the poet, the word may precede the idea; for, as A. N. Whitehead puts it, it is often the case that the poet who could write a lyric on the trees of a forest "concentrates on the trees in order to get at the words."[9]

II *The Path of Chance and Destiny*

Though he is too active to be described as concentrating on trees—in any literal sense—Eberhart has found a quiet home well suited, one may assume, to a poet who would concentrate on the individual's relation to the cosmic rather than on his ties to other men. He has spent the years of his late maturity on the faculty at Dartmouth College, an old, prestigious, and remote school that lacks both the dynamism and the pressures of the multiversities. Driving in mid-March into Hanover, New Hampshire, over the hilly two-lane road still lined with snow banks, a visitor passes only one motel before entering what appears to be the model college town of Hollywood movies.[10] The two-block main street extends from Manchester's garage past Lou's Restaurant, the Village Green, the Dartmouth Bookstore, the Dartmouth Smoke Shop, and, until recent "progress" razed it, the comfortable old Hanover Inn. The street ends at the block-square quadrangle surrounded on three sides by college buildings in a variety of styles: some red brick, one a white oblong with green shutters. In the middle of the quad are the reluctantly melting remnants of a giant snow statue left over from the famous Carnival. The inn had white-jacketed college student waiters, a fireplace with an actual fire in it, a portrait of Daniel Webster (Class of 1801), and large rooms steam heated to insufferability. Villagers and collegians alike stare covertly at the stranger. ("A hundred years," the faculty wife said over her bourbon and water. "In a hundred years Dartmouth will be coeducational.")

We asked the poet why he entered college teaching. He seems to have mixed feelings about this late career. Though he taught in preparatory schools through most of the 1930's and until entering the navy in World War II, he spent the period from 1946 to 1952 with the Butcher Polish Company, manufacturers of wax products. He describes these years in business as a productive, rewarding time when he felt "close to the heart of America" and knew a "dynamism" he has never felt since. He experienced no conflict with poetry; indeed, he thinks that business "may have been more stimulating" than teaching; but he finds that, as a famous poet, "you get your ego patted more" on a campus. The explanation for his turning to teaching is, typically, that he felt "that I was called, almost like a minister used to be."

Eberhart's life, indeed, illustrates his conviction that chance and destiny play a large role in human affairs. Born in Austin, Minnesota, in 1904, he grew up the son of loving, prosperous parents in a small town where he led a conventional boyhood, including attendance at the Congregational Church. He became a leader in high school—captain of the football team, editor of the "annual," president of the Debating League. From about the age of fifteen, he was writing poetry; at least two poems from his teens, "Indian Pipe" and "Burden," survive in *Collected Poems*.

But most of our idylls end. The end, or at least sharp setbacks, came for Eberhart in 1921, when his father (Alpha LaRue Eberhart) began to experience financial difficulty and his mother (Lena Lowenstein Eberhart) began to waste away in what proved to be a long, painful death from lung cancer. His father, a self-made man who had risen to the vice-presidency of the Hormel Meat Packing Company, first suffered reverses when his stock plummeted in value after the discovery that the company had lost one and a quarter million dollars to an embezzler. The financial situation worsened in January, 1922, when he quit in disagreement with the Hormels. The company purchased his stock at its then depressed value, and, though never in poverty, the family was forced to a lower scale of living.

Mrs. Eberhart's illness struck in the summer of 1921, but she did not die until June 22, 1922. While caring for her, almost wishing for her sake that she could die faster, Eberhart became so emotionally involved with the philosophical problems raised by human mortality that they have remained a dominant concern for him. He says, indeed, that the death of his mother made him a poet;[11] however, the pain of his mother's death was somewhat eased by his sense of assurance that there must be a reason for such dying. Neither at this point nor later in his career does Eberhart appear to have developed profound doubts about the values of his upbringing. In his poetry, he is much concerned with mortality; but mortality is a universal problem. His continuing concern is the situation of the individual in the universe, not the welfare of man in society.

Eberhart began his college studies at the University of Minnesota, but after his first year, he transferred, in the fall of 1923, to Dartmouth. Betraying the midwesterner's sense of inferiority toward the East he says: "It was quite a thing for a boy from Minnesota, to come back to Dartmouth." To give details of his career, he moved after dinner to his den, a drafty room, perhaps twelve by twelve feet which is lined with crammed bookshelves and which is furnished with an old couch and a desk piled with papers. After graduating from Dartmouth in 1926, he related,

he heeded his father's desire that he go into business by taking a
job with Marshall Field and Company in Chicago, where he
worked as a basement floorwalker and also wrote "3-line ads
for ladies' undies." During this period he met Harriett Monroe,
the famous editor of *Poetry*, who published eight of his poems
in the November, 1927, issue (XXXI, 80-85). But Eberhart
stayed with Marshall Field only a few months, for he was lured
by an "ideal of poetry"; moreover, he had been admitted to
Cambridge University.

In the 1920's educated young Americans intending to spend a
year or two in Europe often worked their way across the ocean.
Eberhart followed the pattern, but he took the long way around:
he spent from May 25 to the end of September, 1927, knocking
about the Pacific as a deck hand on tramp steamers; but he was
careful enough to have letters of introduction from his father to
businessmen in Pacific ports and shrewd enough to let his shipmates know neither of his passports to respectability nor of his
college education. He says now that he met "man in the raw"
while chipping rust for a living and viewing the port areas of
such cities as Swatow, Hong Kong, and Manila. But his father's
letters also enabled him to meet some of the upper-class citizens
of Asia.

Ironically, the pleasures of his adventuresome wander year
inadvertently came to an end through these connections. A
German ship captain whom he met in Manila agreed to take him
westward as a nonpaying passenger; but two days after the ship
had left port, the second mate ordered Eberhart into the hold
to work as an oiler. When Eberhart protested to the captain,
he discovered that he was in the hands of "a Conrad man—cruel,
vicious, heartless." The captain told him he would have to work
his passage or go overboard. Eberhart thought about leaving the
ship in Borneo, but he stayed on across the Indian Ocean in the
120-degree heat of the ship's hold, bossed around by Germans
who, though "not cruel," were "harsh." Determined not to give
in to the hard work and the heat, he painted ceilings and oiled
machinery; he stayed with the ship as far as Port Said. To
"jump ship" here was not especially risky because he had with
him express checks and a good suit. After two or three "riotous"
days in port, he boarded a British passenger steamer that took
him through the Mediterranean to England, where he arrived after
a voyage made hard by fever that he now thinks was caused by
the "letdown" brought on by relaxation and a clean bed. There
is still an edge in his voice as he speaks of the German captain;

he says that he wanted to "get justice against" him, but the
process would have taken too much time.

Arriving in England on October 14, 1927, he entered Saint
John's College, Cambridge; a small legacy from his mother
provided his support. Among his tutors was F. R. Leavis; and I. A.
Richards, already famous, encouraged his writing. Eberhart has
maintained friendship with Richards, who visited him in Hanover
in 1966. At Cambridge, Eberhart "came into my own as a
poet," though he had been "in a poetic circle" while at Dartmouth. He was the only American in a group of classmates
that included William Empson, Kathleen Raine, and T. H.
White. It was, he says, a "most heady time." He took a course
in Aristotle's poetics from Arthur Quiller-Couch; he was impressed by the proximity of A. E. Housman though he stayed
away from him because of his reputation for wanting no for-
eigners around; and he caught an occasional glimpse of Ludwig
Wittgenstein, the philosopher. That Eberhart admired poets,
critics, and philosophers probably helps explain the apparent
ease with which he was later drawn into college teaching.

He took both parts of the English Tripos and received his
Cambridge bachelor's degree in 1929 (with the passage of time
and payment of the required fee, he received his master's in
1933). Meanwhile, he had vacationed in London; Ireland, where,
in the summer of 1928, he met Yeats; Spain; and Majorca "when
few Americans had been there." When he graduated, things were
"on top of the world"; but in the fall of 1929 the great stock-
market crash not only gave his family another blow but also
removed prospects of easy employment. Unable to find the job
in publishing which he thought his education entitled him to,
Eberhart worked for three months in a slaughterhouse and wrote
a few book reviews. He then took a job tutoring two daughters
of the Rodney Proctor family—the wealthy soap makers—in
Palm Beach, Florida, from December, 1929, to April, 1930. In the
summer of 1930, while staying at the Foster cottage in Phoenix-
ville, Pennsylvania, he saw the dead animal that he later wrote
about in "The Groundhog."

In 1928 and 1929 he had been writing the long poem that
became A Bravery of Earth, which was published in London
early in 1930 and appeared in the United States later that year;
but a first book of poetry does not earn many men a living.
In September, 1930, Eberhart was appointed to tutor the son of
the king of Siam, then visiting the United States, because, he
explains, he appealed to the court as an American with an

English accent and education (and, he adds, a cane, spats, and a mustache). This assignment "took care" of him for about a year in 1930 and 1931; one result of his experience was the poem "The Rape of the Cataract."

Eberhart had made good money working for the Siamese, and he wanted to learn German. In October, 1931, he went to Berlin for a year, learning German "pretty well." During the year, he spent some time on the ski slopes; and he also visited Stuttgart where his ancestors had "ruled for centuries" (the city still has an Eberhartstrasse). One ancestor came to Pennsylvania in 1725, and the Eberhart lineage includes "many stern Protestant" forefathers. He says that, while in Germany, he did not know what was happening in the political world; for, "I regret to say, I've never been a politically oriented man." He regards himself as meditative rather than political; but, he says, he has been "healthy and physically active"—an opinion easily accepted by a visitor two decades younger who had trouble keeping up with him as he ran up a Baker library stairway. After Eberhart returned to the United States about the end of 1932, it took him, he says, another ten years to realize what Nazism was.

At the time, he thought that the only thing he did not have that he might want was a doctoral degree, which he supposed would give him security. Moreover, he "had done so well at Cambridge" that he was lured on. He entered the Harvard graduate school in the fall of 1932, but he dropped out in 1933 because by then the depression in the United States was "almost frightening." Single and well educated, he did not have economic difficulties as serious as those of many men in depression-time America. But, though nonpolitical, he was not insensitive; and he responded to the times both in his poetry and in his career choices. He had made straight A's in George Lyman Kittredge's Shakespeare classes, he had studied under Irving Babbitt, and he had talked with T. S. Eliot and admired Alfred North Whitehead. But, to be able to stay another two or three years in graduate school, he would have had to borrow thousands of dollars that he could see no possibility of repaying. Quitting graduate study, he took a teaching job in 1933 at Saint Mark's School in Southborough, Massachusetts, where he stayed until 1940. His attitude that Saint Mark's was desirable only for the paycheck it gave him shows in his remark that "I rode out the Depression in this fancy Episcopal boys' school for eight years."

The years at Saint Mark's were not without other rewards. One student who brought poetry to him for advice was Robert

Lowell. Asked if, in his teaching, he has produced many poets, Eberhart says that a man is probably lucky if in a career he has one student with real talent. Eberhart also became acquainted with W. H. Auden, already well known; and he helped arrange a one-month position for Auden as a visiting teacher at Saint Mark's in 1938. But Eberhart's career did not seem to be advancing. Editors still dealt him more rejection slips than acceptances, even though he published during these years *Reading the Spirit* (1937) and wrote many of the poems that later appeared in *Song and Idea* (1942).

"My basic drive," he says, "was always to be a poet. But in those days there were not the possibilities of recognition that there are today." Eberhart's applications for Guggenheim fellowships were rejected several times, despite support from well-known poets and critics. His spirits were not improved by a long period of unsuccessful job hunting that followed notice from Saint Mark's that, effective in December, 1940, the school's budget would not allow it to retain him.

But circumstances outside his career began to improve. Through her brother Charles Butcher, Jr., who had come to Saint Mark's to teach, he had met Helen Elizabeth Butcher. They were married on August 29, 1941. He finally found another job, this one at Cambridge School in Kendall Green, Massachusetts, and he began teaching there in the fall of 1941. But World War II was already in progress. As America began to arm, Eberhart took a period of military training; and, after Pearl Harbor, he began to seek a more desirable assignment than the lottery of Selective Service might give him. In fact, as he told me, because of his age he might not have been called to serve. But he was patriotic, and when he learned of a chance to use his teaching experience, he took a commission in the Naval Reserve in August, 1942, to serve as a gunnery instructor. His duty stations included posts in Florida; at Dam Neck, Virginia; in New Jersey; and at Alameda on San Francisco Bay. Remaining on duty in the Bay area as an officer administrator for some months after the end of the war, he led an active social and literary life, associating with Kenneth Rexroth and other writers and giving public readings.

When he was discharged in the spring of 1946, Elizabeth—"Betty"—was pregnant. Eberhart joined the Butcher firm; he was enthusiastic, he says, because it seemed "more realistic" than teaching. He held several administrative posts with the company; meanwhile, he continued his poetic career and received

at last a fair measure of approval from critics, as well as a number
of prizes. He was still working for the company in the early 1950's
when he was busily engaged with the Poets' Theatre.

But Eberhart's interest in writing made campus life attractive
to him, and in 1952 he took a leave from the polish company
to accept a visiting professorship at the University of Washington
as a one-year replacement while Theodore Roethke went on
leave. Eberhart then taught for a year at the University of
Connecticut, another year at Wheaton College, and still another
year at Princeton. Dartmouth had given him an honorary degree
in 1954, and in 1955, while he was at Princeton, Dartmouth's
president and "whole administration" asked him to come to
Hanover. He has remained at Dartmouth since the fall of 1956,
receiving tenure in 1958. He has taken occasional leaves, one to
return to Seattle as visiting professor in the spring of 1967. He
also spent "two marvellous years" (1959-61) as consultant in
poetry at the Library of Congress, one under the Eisenhower
administration and one under John Kennedy ("my kind of man").
At Dartmouth, as professor of English and poet in residence,
he teaches two classes in the fall and usually only one in the
spring. He has a voice in the English Department decisions on
hiring and firing faculty members; and, though not obligated
to serve on all college committees, he takes assignments to arrange for visits by poets (among those he has helped bring to
the campus have been Marianne Moore, W. H. Auden, Robert
Frost, and Dylan Thomas). He remains a member of the board
of directors and an honorary vice-president for Butcher Polish.
He also leads an active career reading his poetry on the platform.

The Eberhart house in Hanover is about a mile from the
main street, an old, white two-story frame building at the end
of a street with neighbors only on the north. Tall pines surround the house on the other three sides. The land to the west
falls off rather steeply down to the Connecticut River, and
Vermont lies on its far side. The furnishings are somewhat worn,
and there is an accumulation of odds and ends, for comfort
and family living are valued. Mrs. Eberhart is the courteous
hostess; and the poet, smoking a pipe, converses with the polite
alertness that characterizes his responses to questions at a public
reading. He talks of their summer home, "Undercliff," a salt-water
farm under a three-hundred foot cliff some seventeen miles from
the village of Bluehill, Maine. One of Eberhart's activities
there is flying the kites which he writes about in several poems.

Another is sailing in the thirty-six foot boat, *Reve*; this is the boat, from which ashes are strewn in the poem "Sea Burial from the Cruiser *Reve*."

He discusses freely his forthright use of generalizations, his unabashed employment of abstractions, and his moralizing. In the first place, "We are what we are as poets," he says, "for very profound and subtle reasons." One may be fated to be a poet and thus have a very strong will—"which I think I've always had"—but one cannot account for this. At any rate, he adds, "I knew I was a poet by the time I was over at Cambridge . . . I knew I really had something." One may take Alexander Pope as an example, he suggests; for everything Pope says is moralizing. As for his own beliefs, he says, "I don't have a platform." He is a "meliorist," grew up "ambivalent," and "Never can make up my mind about anything"; indeed, he feels that he could not continue to write if he had a set platform.

On the matter of religion, Eberhart says "I'm an Episcopalian, but with some kind of a difference." He was reared a Congregationalist, but chapel every day at Saint Mark's "made me in love with the Episcopal service." He is not on the church records, however, though he says that his wife is and that she tells him he is not honest because he does not enroll. "I think I'm a Christian," he says, but he admits that he is "not a great churchgoer." He observes that editors have found several of his poems, such as "The Horse Chestnut Tree," to be religious verse.

In Eberhart's view, "All great poets must generalize"; if "our time doesn't think so, it shows how far we've lapsed from greatness." Eberhart regards Marianne Moore as an "adorable" person; "we have movies of her here." But her work leaves him "cold" because it has "no passion." This age, indeed, is so crass that a "spiritual poetry" is denied whereas "near prose" such as hers will succeed. The Picasso-like poets, he says, are "afraid of the depths of life and afraid to generalize." Charles Tomlinson, for example, is strict in particularizing and thus cannot put fire into a poem: his writing is precise, crystalline, excellent; but it has "not enough generalization." He adds that "Even W. C. Williams got over that." And "Old man Frost, who's sat in this room quite a few times, tells you in a general way" (Eberhart uses "old" half affectionately as well as descriptively for such poets as Frost and Robinson Jeffers, men born two decades before he was). As for Eberhart himself, he went through a phase in the 1940's when he doubted any "grand generalization" because he thought it might have a falseness, a sentimentality, to it. The danger of such error is greater for those who generalize than for the "poets of the miniscule." But, he says, some of the greatest poets of the present era are great because they are "daring"—for example, W. H. Auden in his poem on the death of Yeats. Ezra Pound is not much good at generalization; moreover, for this reason, among others, his *Cantos* are "such a pasticherie" that they lack "force of generalization" and hence have much "wind" and a "shaky overall architecture." Eberhart does not think that in his own poetry he moralizes too much: perhaps "moral poetry is the only kind that endures," poetry "that conduces to the good of mankind." Man, being a social animal, wants that to endure which is good for him. No one would want to imitate the lives of Rimbaud, Baudelaire, Van Gogh, or Dylan Thomas. But the poetry of these men gives "an elevated spirit" to a reader. Eberhart, indeed, can hardly imagine an immoral poem (one possible exception is a "pornographic poem"). Even François Villon, though realistic and getting to "the base of life," is "cleansing" to read.

About the "Beats" of the 1950's and early 1960's Eberhart is on the whole approving, perhaps partly because he thinks of himself as something of a discoverer; for his piece in the *New York Times* served to introduce them to a new audience.[12] One result of this article was a twenty-five-page letter from Allen Ginsberg, who was then writing "Howl." Eberhart thinks Ginsberg has a profoundly religious mind, a "terrific spiritual energy." He is neutral about Lawrence Ferlinghetti, but says "I like his poetry." He remarks that Ferlinghetti drew a thousand students to a reading at Dartmouth, almost the largest crowd such readings have drawn. He speculates on why Ferlinghetti has not won approval of "the Establishment." And what is that? He does not know but supposes he belongs to it himself. Ferlinghetti's poetry has seemed "so easy, imitative, not too profound"; he has drawn a large audience but is "not thought to be a an incisive mind" and "Tate wouldn't think much of him." The "Beat" movement, at any rate, became "meretricious" because success arrived too rapidly. Eberhart thinks that it was a "fascinating sociological phenomenon," that it had thousands of people interested in poetry, and that for that reason it "was mighty fine." In these comments, as in his activity at the Library of Congress, Eberhart shows a sense of professionalism, a feeling that what is good for poetry as an institution is to be approved.

Another "sociological mystery" to Eberhart is the short-lived
movement in the 1940's and 1950's for a verse drama. Eberhart,
who is proud of his role in this development, is sorry that it died.
Lyon Phelps began the Poets' Theatre in 1950, broaching the
idea to Eberhart, Violet Lang, John Ciardi, Robert Lowell,
Archibald MacLeish, Thornton Wilder, and others. Eberhart
says, "We all thought it was going to be the Abbey Theater, at
least"; and it was "very potent" for a short while. The founders
dispersed, Ciardi going to Rutgers and Eberhart himself to
Washington. The group "never made any money, to speak of,"
drawing its biggest profit ($2,000) for a reading by some of the
Sitwells. One of its enterprises was what was probably the first
reading of Dylan Thomas's unfinished "Under Milkwood," ten
days before the reading at the Young Men's Hebrew Association
in New York that has been cited as the first. The only "bigtime
success" in verse drama besides that of T. S. Eliot was Archibald
MacLeish's *Job*, a play that was "too big" for the group. Repeating
that the Poets' Theatre was an "exciting social phenomenon,"
Eberhart says that he has "Never felt since the excitement of a
belief that it [verse drama] is necessary to life."

The reader of Eberhart's work quickly becomes aware that
he is not a follower of William Carlos Williams, Ezra Pound,
Robert Frost, or any of the other influential figures in the generation immediately preceding his own. He says that his work
resembles Frost's only "here and there." His early poem "Burden,"
about a hill near Hanover, is "a little bit Frostian"; but, on the
whole, "I don't think I'm influenced by him." He came to know
Frost only in the last year's of the elder poet's life. He did have
"two friendships with older poets," Williams and Stevens.
Eberhart feels that briefly in the later 1940's his work exhibited
some similarity to that of Stevens, but he doubts that it amounted
to much. The Dartmouth library has thirty-five letters exchanged
between Eberhart and Stevens in the period 1948 to 1955.[13]
Speaking of them, Eberhart sums up Stevens's position as a
belief that there is no imitation; that each poet is his own man.
Not poets of this century but Wordsworth, Blake, and perhaps
Gerard Manley Hopkins are, Eberhart feels, his real poetic
ancestors.

Not an influence but an admired figure, perhaps because of
his independence, was Robinson Jeffers. Eberhart said that he
has always respected Jeffers's work and once when visiting
Carmel he called him up though he knew that he "resisted seeing

people." He found to his pleasure that Jeffers knew his work, and Eberhart gladly visited with the "grand old man" for two hours.

At breakfast, Mrs. Eberhart was out on an early errand; and the son and daughter had left for class. Eberhart, as host, went back and forth from the round table in front of the black Franklin stove to the toaster on the counter. The table holds a candlestick, made by Mrs. Eberhart, in the shape of banyan roots and one of her clay pots. Eberhart served rosehaw jam with the toast and discussed the politics of poetry. The National Book Award to James Dickey had just been announced, and Eberhart had expected that it might come to him for *Selected Poems 1930-1965* (1965). But he said only that maybe his "turn" will come, a comment that again shows his attitude that poetry is an institution with certain proprieties.

III   *The Poet as Mature Professional*

The achievement of a poet in our time is recorded on the printed page. But in the last two decades poets have often also published by giving public readings of their work. Eberhart is a skilled reader, thoroughly professional in choice of material, audience appeal, and delivery; and, at the same time, respectful of the art he is practicing. In public presentation he typically mixes comment about poetic art with remarks on his own aims, and observations about the origin and development of some of the poems he reads. One attending a reading by Eberhart therefore has a literary experience and also learns much incidental information about the poet's practices.

At one reading not long ago, speaking from the temporary wooden stage in the red-draped, white and gold Imperial Room of the Americana Hotel on a chill, dripping New York December night, Eberhart won a standing ovation from his audience of some two hundred members of the Modern Language Association.[14] It was a triumph for him that they rose, for they were wearied by long sitting on folding chairs; and their attention had been sought by a noisily publicized meeting in the ballroom across the hall of some five hundred members seeking to "radicalize" the association. Alert, quick in his replies to questions, skillfully modulating his voice for effective delivery of his poetic lines, Eberhart had held his audience by force of personality and by genial humor. A man in his sixties of no more than medium height, perhaps five feet eight inches tall, and stocky in build, he is balding though he has a fringe of white on the

sides of his head, and his eyes are of the brightness that a magazine writer would call "electric." He is, in short, a poet who
himself exemplifies the ebullient vigor of the man who speaks in
most of his poems.

Eberhart began his reading by sketching a few principles: the
inner life is stronger than the outer; life is ultimately mysterious;
poetry defends individualism. He quoted R. Buckminster Fuller,
the industrial designer, as an authority for the view that poetry
is valuable because it generalizes and evaluates. Still citing
Fuller, Eberhart said that science too often bogs men down in
particularities. The audience accepted these assertions not as
points of argument to be analyzed but as guideposts—indications
of the direction the poet's work will follow.

The expected introductory remarks completed, Eberhart and
the audience were glad to turn to the purpose of the evening: the
reading of a score of poems. He first read three that exemplify
some of his beliefs and practices. " 'Go to the Shine That's on a
Tree' " shows his desperate insistence on taking a cue from the
glory that he believes may speak to us through nature. "The
Illusion of Eternity," a fairly late poem, gives a similar though
much chastened affirmation: the sensory appeals of nature are
an illusion, for they seem to show a world that shares in eternity
though wisdom tells us that the world in actuality knows suffering and struggle; yet illusions are "acceptable." Another
fairly late poem, "Hardening into Print," speaks of aiming to
catch the "meaning" of life, while remaining open to other
mysteries as well; of expressing the "immaculate joy" of a glimpse
into understanding despite awareness of "human ills." With these
readings, Eberhart introduced himself as a man sobered but not
defeated by maturity.

Knowing that his audience was comprised of teachers, many of
whom use some of the poems in class, he commented on the
origins and purposes of sixteen favorite poems. He called " 'When
Doris Danced' " a light poem, perhaps somewhat like seven-
teenth-century verse; and, laughing, he brought out its slight
bawdiness by remarking that he gets "a lot of mileage" out of its
last syllable (which he reads with emphasis). "For a Lamb" came
to him after he saw a dead animal one spring while he was
studying at Cambridge University. The poem is a "postal card
of the world" and, if it is "read one way," then "easily you can
see the transcendentalism behind it." This theme led him on
for five years through "what mysteries I still don't understand"
to "The Groundhog," a poem that, he said, he could not read on

the platform for many years because he did not want to be known as a poet of only one poem. About composition of this poem, he remarked that personality is a "vehicle for spirit," that the piece came to him by inspiration in fifteen minutes. The audience was sympathetic as he reported that the manuscript was lost and that he would like to compare it with the existing version.

Of " 'If I Could Only Live at the Pitch that Is Near Madness' " he said, "in retrospect, it was my way out of the Depression." At that time one could "have no way out" in the world of society and was forced inward. For himself, he "posited . . . a vision of the perfection of the world and of life." The poem owes something to Wordsworth's "Ode"; and he explained that the "madness" it speaks of is not pathological but "the divine frenzy of the Greeks." The poem "New Hampshire, February" was based on an incident that took place during his bachelor days when he was spending a week studying and writing in a house near Exeter, New Hampshire.[15] One day two wasps happened to fall from the ceiling where they had apparently been hibernating and landed on the edge of the stove. He "innocently"—that is, more or less inadvertently—pushed them to the center of the stove, where the heat woke them up. Seeing that they might sting him, he moved them to the edge of the stove where they quieted once again. Interested in this observation, he again warmed the insects to activity and then cooled them. One fell off and was accidentally killed by his boot. The audience laughed as he said "I'd been reading Schopenhauer, Nietzsche, and Thomas Hardy." He commented that, though "a couple" of poems have come to him on the spur of the moment, most have come later when he is in "a curious higher state of being"; and this poem came to him some months after the incident. He observed that in the poem he altered the circumstances slightly by using his breath to warm the insects and having them in a pan instead of simply on top of the stove.

One of the two pieces in *Collected Poems* (1960) that came to him instantly was "The Groundhog." The other one was "The Cancer Cells." It happened, he says, that on a hot August day in Newark, New Jersey, he took a room in the Military Park Hotel, because he had been amused by its name. In his room he opened a copy of *Life* to a double-page spread of cancer cells "so lethal and so beautiful" that they suggested thought of "Keat's truth and beauty . . . this dichotomy." After presenting the poem, he read for the humor of it, "since most of us are teachers," a schoolboy theme preposterously "interpreting" the poem as a warning against the spread of communism.

He introduced "The Horse Chestnut Tree" as a poem written a couple of years after World War II when he was living in Cambridge, Massachusetts, in his father-in-law's house. The tree, standing in the yard, attracted raids by boys; and since his father-in-law was aging, Eberhart promised one spring that he would handle the raiders. When the boys came, he went out; for "I never felt more that I was right." But when a boy he grabbed started to yell "Police, police" Eberhart let him go and went back into the house. The boys, he came to realize, were "estheticians," were "Plato's lovers of the beautiful." The more he thought about the boys, the more he liked them. He got his "revenge" on them six months later by writing the poem.

He began his presentation of "The Fury of Aerial Bombardment" by quoting Auden's statement (in "In Memory of W. B. Yeats") that poetry makes nothing happen. This is true only "politically," Eberhart observed; for poetry "does something in subtle ways." He believes with I. A. Richards that poetry "helps sharpen insights," "makes us better people," and "modifies the structures of the past by imposing new structures on them." Holding these beliefs while thinking about World War II, he said that he believes it was a "just war" but that he is aware of doubts. As instances of "pessimism" about the war, he mentioned Henry Reed's "The Naming of Parts" and Randall Jarrell's "Death of the Ball Turret Gunner." For himself, he "never could square . . . with Christianity" the fact that he had "taught thousands of young men to kill firing machine guns," an allusion to his wartime assignment as a navy aerial gunnery instructor. One day while sitting on barracks steps at Dam Neck, Virginia, he saw on the "hoardings" the names of his students listed. Some of them had died within three weeks after leaving him. He wrote the first twelve lines of the poem as a prayer, he said, and then put it away for two weeks. He then wrote the concluding four lines in "a cool way." The mention in the poem's opening of "silent" spaces is, he added, an echo of Pascal's concern about the silence of the stars. Remarking that he has written twenty to twenty-five war poems, he read "Evil," a poem opposing the Vietnam war which he first read on November 11, 1967.

Eberhart next read several of his newer poems, opening with "Ball Game" because, he said, it is of the "metaphysical" type that is sometimes identified with him. He read "Santa Claus in Oaxaca" because the incongruity of the situation struck him as "really quite wonderful . . . in a civilization far older than ours." Another, "The Ides of March," is "One I like because it has a musical flow." In New England, he said, one spends "a lot of time going by graveyards." He wrote this poem "a couple of years ago . . . and I guess I like what it says." After reading "On Returning to a Lake in Spring," he introduced "A Wedding on Cape Rosier" by giving information on its circumstances. Cape Rosier is near the Eberhart family's summer home. The Father (Kendall) Emerson mentioned in the poem remembered Emily Dickinson as a woman who made a pet of him and wrote him poems in the years when he was six to nine years old. The audience was pleased to hear that Father Emerson gave Eberhart three recollections about Miss Dickinson—that it is true that she dressed in white, that she was a good-looking woman, and that she made very good doughnuts.

Another new poem, "Outwitting the Trees," is a piece that Eberhart asserted "bespeaks the mystery of poetry." It is based on the "magnificent" trees around his house that grow "about 100 feet tall" (in the poem, he says eighty feet tall). A poem "of a new nature for me" is "Marrakech," which is "just long lines that tell a description of a dance." He described the "fabulous place," the marketplace in Marrakech, Morocco, near the twelfth-century Koutubia tower where storytellers and snake charmers entertain. The dancers described in the poem are men reared in the High Atlas Mountains, who carry on a practice that has lasted for six hundred years in the same spot. "Think of that," he said, "in comparison with the history of this country."

As an encore, Eberhart read "On a Squirrel Crossing the Road in Autumn, in New England," a poem that has "a little tag at the end." When the incident which gave rise to the poem occurred, he had feared that he had hit the squirrel with his car and had pulled to the side of the road. Though he saw that he had missed the animal, he had sat for a while "terribly nerved up," in a state of "clairvoyance" in which "I felt every possible connection with the little creature." This poem and "The Cancer Cells" are the two pieces in *Collected Poems* that were written immediately after the incidents that gave rise to them.

Throughout the presentation Eberhart read clearly and in a voice that carried to all the audience. This professional skill, together with his selection of poems and his informative, often humorous comments, kept the audience with him; and, when he invited questions, several were posed. When someone asked about the length of the title of "On a Squirrel Crossing the Road in Autumn, in New England," Eberhart answered that it is "just a description." When someone else asked why his British publishers had wanted to omit the ending half line, the poet replied that he could only speculate, that perhaps it was because "even to this day the British are behind us in poetry," that they "still think poetry should be regular in meter." When another voice asked whether poems came to him partly "as rhythm," Eberhart said that he thinks so, that he once woke up in the morning with a line going through his head, "The river of sweetness that runs through the meadow of lies." When he wrote the poem "Hill Dream of Youth, Thirty Years Later," he used that line and published it in *The Atlantic* and later in *Shifts of Being* (1968).

When someone raised a better question—Would he read another poem?—Eberhart read a recent one, "Van Black, a Farmer in His Dell." Asked to read "Cover Me Over," he thumbed the pages to find it, meanwhile remarking that it is on the gravestones of three members of his family, that it may eventually be on others, and that it can be thought of as "just a sleep song." After the ovation, he read one more poem, "Throwing the Apple," which he said he had been pleased to see discussed in a recent issue of *Explicator*.[16] Explaining that the poem is based on D. H. Lawrence's painting *Throwing Back the Apple,* he stated that he had always admired Lawrence.

The whole performance had a relaxed seriousness that kept the audience at ease and did not detract from the poetry. Perhaps because he has given readings for more than two decades, Eberhart is able to present his own poems as though they were somewhat separate from himself, to keep the focus on them rather than on himself. But one also sees Eberhart's thorough professionalism: he honors poetry enough to treat it seriously, to respect it as a work of art instead of seeing it as merely an expression of its author's feelings. Certainly, the reading was evidence that Eberhart's predilections are for what he terms "the healthy psyche" rather than the sick psyche. One may contrast his performance with the entirely egocentric reading of Allen Ginsberg, a poet who becomes so hypnotized by his own words that he forgets any audience before him and who certainly would regard his verse as inseparable from his sensitive self.

At the end of the Eberhart reading, a few audience members went to the platform. The rest went into the lobby, mixing inadvertently with the larger crowd just emerging from the radicals' meeting. Like the current of the Amazon that is said

to retain its hues for a hundred miles or more even after flowing
into the ocean, Eberhart's audience members in their conventional dress could have been easily distinguished from the
hairily uniform would-be radicals. Eberhart himself is a liberal—
a man who is as opposed as the radicals to politico-military
adventuring and to race prejudice—but he does not therefore
demand that all life be dominated by politics. The sort of radicalism Eberhart might properly be identified with is that of
what he would call the spirit, the radicalism of the individual
confronting destiny. This confrontation is the continuing theme
of his poetry.

CHAPTER 2

The Seeker of a Bravery

S TUDY of Eberhart's volumes of poetry in chronological order shows that the esthetic positions and practices of his most mature work express an adulthood that, indeed, grew up by a process of maturation. His first book is the long, partly autobiographical *A Bravery of Earth* (1930). Besides its minor function as an exercise—a relatively free and relaxed composition allowing him to experiment with a variety of modes—it has the major purpose of exploring the neo-Romantic assumptions he held in the beginning of his career. It ends in a triumphant declaration of determination to seize a "bravery." Yet it hints at the nature of the resolutions he would develop, at later acceptance of hard "knowledge" and recognition of claims of the flesh. The poems in *Reading the Spirit* (1936) and *Song and Idea* (1942) are written as additional declarations of youthful exuberance, but they also express recognitions of "knowledge"; and they all but declare the interinvolvement of flesh and spirit that the poems of Eberhart's middle period openly proclaim. The reliance on love and assurance of immortality that characterize his later work are not strong in his earliest compositions, but they are seen as possibilities. A continuing motive is the search for unity, as a continuing resolution to perplexity is declaration of "mystery." His ideas about all these fundamentals develop as his career progresses.

I *Declaring Nobility*: A Bravery of Earth

The autobiographical *A Bravery of Earth* (1930) is a prelude, an investigation and presentation of influences that have shaped the ideas and feelings of a young poet. In this aim, it parallels Wordsworth's intentions in *The Prelude*;[1] and, like Wordsworth's poem, *A Bravery of Earth* includes many passages dealing with events that parallel incidents of the author's own life, though one is not to assume that there is always a direct relationship

between statements in the poem and events of the poet's life. One recognizes a similarity also in the use of such material as the Platonic doctrine of "recollection," the idea that a man comes to this earth as a new embodiment of preexisting energies. But Wordsworth published his poem in his maturity, when he could assess and sometimes judiciously alter passages written earlier; Eberhart printed his work while still a young man, and it shows the heat and uncertainties of the talented beginner. Eberhart's concern, moreover, it not with how a man may find solace through nature but with how he may endure and win a measure of "bravery". Assuming that death is an event of significance, not simply an end to existence, he asks what this significance may be; and he alternately exults, cries out, and meditates as he ponders the question of how man should confront destiny.

Eberhart's speaker opens by celebrating a youthful fervor of mystery. Though the young poet recognizes that sobering age will come, he holds thought of it in abeyance. Central to the passage are lines 5 and 6, in which he speaks of the "secret hallowing" that "fevers" him as "Mystery made visible/ In growth, yet subtly veiled in all. . . ." The sensory delights of spring express a force in experience which he can recognize but cannot comprehend, which nature symbolizes but does not explain. His use of "regenerate" and "incarnation," as well as "hallowing," suggests a religious, if not specifically Christian, basis for his fervor. Rapturous moments are brief, for life is a "quick kaleidoscope" that shuffles one between summery wonder and wintery doubt. Recognizing doubt and mortality, the poet knows that he is naked in the universe. This knowledge comes early in life, by intuition or by strong feeling rather than from maturation. Even as a youth he must be aware of the "supreme indifference," of the universe's refusal to reveal any purposes it may have for the individual.

Like Wordsworth, Eberhart's poet sees three stages of philosophical or esthetic existence paralleling man's growth from childhood through youth to early adulthood. In man's first stage, the child, arriving as a "spark of . . . new, ancient life," as a newborn human being and as a representative of an "insistent" life force or "will," lives in a "simple awareness" of the world about him. Man moves through the second stage into the third, the young adulthood in which he achieves "the first perilous understanding" of his destiny. Much of the poem's first fifty-two pages is a celebration of the second stage—the youth during which man experiences "the spacious interval/ Of eager animal

harmony." In this period, vitality wells up within him as he seems for a time to exist in perfect harmony of will and physical nature. This is the time for love, for the fevering exulted over in the opening lines of the poem. Returning to Platonic speculation on preexistence, "the long enduring that is before/ Awareness," the speaker feels in himself a new effort of the will to understand itself, an individual summoned from the apparently boundless past. As an adult looking back, the poet recognizes that he lived in illusions during youth, that his joys with a girl were inadequate, a "Love without idea." He realizes that he was dominated by the moon, associated with lovely illusions, but that as a man he is subject to the sun, a burning clarity.

The first impact of sun is a sense of rebirth, of joys continued but deepened. Youth concedes that it can know nothing of a universal power that may watch over man. But he is almost lyrical in declaring that man, "This dust of stars," must hail something beyond the death that he knows waits for him. In a last bravado, the youth defies doubt by asserting his sense that there is harmony in the universe. For the moment, he can be as optimistic as Whitman. He knows death will come, yet he is sure that grass will continue to grow, that "What man calls death is only/ Change. . . ."

In the midst of this optimism that even the youth recognizes as perfervid, night brings premonitions that cause him to see his previous exultations as unreal; and he welcomes the chaos that he had once confidently denied. He has entered the "second awareness," the adulthood in which there will appear to be not a harmony in experience but a division between illusions and reality. Validity existed in the child's sense of perfection and in the youth's search for values and for God; but the new awareness brought the reality also of doubt, despair, pain. In a series of proselike assertions, the poet declares that perfection and mere being are passive, that the right goal is "to become." For a time, he tells us, everything in him but the life energy itself seemed to die. He resigned himself to dependence upon reason rather than upon insight, to a world of grayness where futility replaces meaning. He tried briefly to urge himself to a life of unthinking but forceful action. Trying next to imitate the stars' tranquillity, he found himself still enmeshed in human suffering. In a passage reminiscent of what may have been Eberhart's own feelings as his mother lay dying of cancer, the poet meditates upon the recognition of harshness forced by observation of a lengthy, pain-

ful death. Now not only the moon of youth but also the sun of early adulthood were powerless, and the poet wished to be one with nothingness.

These prosaic pages lead to more vivid passages upon experience at a funeral. Deciding that life is "dust and shadows only," the poet despairingly reflected on the "counter-will" that had blighted him, the creation of "triumph-will." This "counter-will" brought him a sense of corruption in life. Yet he can, after a pause, describe himself as beyond bitterness, as impersonally watching the cancerous powers that consume man. Loneliness, the futility of heroic action and of art and thought—these contribute to the "vast oblivion of the living" that the poet sees at the end of the poem's long first section.

The second section of the poem (56-65) reports the speaker's decision to become an artist, a decision which is shown, not as the consequence of a compulsion nor as of a moment of conversion, but as a deliberate act of the will. He made the choice in order to escape chaos, to find freedom through creation of form. He climbs the hill of art, the home of an absolute beauty appearing in the objects of nature, the forms the artist would imitate. At times he is tempted to rise only to a height at which he feels a kinship with the great dead (both those of the past, and those yet to live) and with nature itself. But he climbs on, determined to explore the dualisms, indeed the complexities, that he once thought chaotic but now knows to be part of existence. He reflects that, though the sun brings an overflow of feeling, the will creates the "urge to art"; and he ascends to peaks where he becomes a "tingling and visionary being." At this height, he sees five Greeks (apparently, Homer, Prometheus, Socrates, Plato, and Aristotle). Other figures also appear, among them Michelangelo and Nietzsche, the latter celebrated as one who shouted "what mankind might strive to become." But, finding this height too rarefied, the poet returns to his fellow men. One gathers that, though he feels that he cannot match the achievements of the greatest artists and thinkers, he is determined to equal or exceed the usual accomplishments of the talented.

The third section (65-71) opens with an apostrophe urging the mind to find a way to harmonize the delights man's senses give him with the darkness and the doubt that come from his knowledge of mortality. The poet finds that moments of absolute vacancy come, when the mind perceives neither the sun of delight nor the shadow of doubt, and the very objects that at other times give rise to sensations seem to exist only in the brain.

In this stage, when one concludes that "The objects one senses are in the mind," the mind becomes "the conqueror of life." A unity is imposed, but it is meaningless, a merely static and terrifying blankness. Such "Willed annihilation" breeds a terror in which there is neither certainty nor doubt, only promise of death. The poet throws himself upon the stars and sun, struggling to go beyond the human to "the full impersonal" where he senses the unity of man and stone with the sun. The passage, artfully repeating the words "Out of astounding gloom," serves as a transition to the lyricism of the section's last forty-seven lines, which despite some dated Romanticism of diction ("gays" as a verb) and syntax ("And all is ravage") is a fine celebration of the intuition as an instrument for releasing "Imagination's elation."

The ascent of the hill foreshadowed the long voyage over the Pacific and through the Indian Ocean which provides the narrative thread for the quest that is related in the fourth section of the poem (72-127). The section opens with a passage in highly artificial syntax, perhaps intended to be reminiscent of Hopkins. Filled with capitalized terms for the mysteriously spiritual ("the Far," the "Near," the "Lovely Away," the "Beyond Profound"), it leads to a declaration that "There is a purpose to be found/ Finding . . . "—a statement acceptable as an indication of the poet's motive (if only because one recognizes that men do act upon such bases). Like a migratory bird, the young man of the poem sets out for home—the Orient, the source of spiritual inspiration. He goes to California and ships out as a deck hand to Asia. The poem characterizes half a dozen of his shipmates, describes the alternating feelings of desolation and glory that come to an imaginative man standing night watches on the ocean, and recounts details of brutal sensory experience as the ship enters the heat of the tropics.

Some of the poem's better passages are in these characterizations and descriptions, probably because Eberhart draws exact details from the voyage he made in 1927. The ship takes him from China to the Philippines and on to Southeast Asia, and the poet occasionally returns to his question, "Where's reality?" He seeks the mystic's goal, the state

> Beyond vicissitudes and stings;
> Without memory, or hope;
> Without desire, at its core;
> Beyond belief, beyond joy, . . .

The characterizations anticipate Eberhart's later turn to poetic drama and to such pieces as "The Tobacconist of Eighth Street."

Resolution comes finally, not as the solution to a logical problem, but as a realization of the poet's participation in the godlike energy which he postulates as the active principle in the universe. Sexual imagery of driving pistons leads to lines describing a quiet sea off the coast of Africa where, though still without the stars he had sought, the poet realizes that work in the intense heat of the engine room is comparable to mankind's struggle under the fires of the sun. A storm reinforces the analogy of shipboard labor to the heroic struggles of a man's life, and the poet becomes aware, through intuition, that there is an identity in the universe: "A man stark naked firing a boiler!/ A god in the hell-hole of a ship!" The fireman is urged to wield a shovel like a god attempting to feed the demoniacal earth with time, to work so furiously to feed the furnaces that he becomes himself "a thing/ Of fire! fire-like!" This state, the poet finally declares, is "the splendid reincarnation." Man, if he imitates the gods by heroic action may, one gathers, become like them. Understanding this possibility enables one to surpass youth, to achieve a maturity in which "man stands up/ In a bravery of earth." This achievement is as glorious as the sunfire that sets grass glowing in the spring, that "fevers" the poet with sensory delight and with desire for understanding. This attainment is not a triumph over time, because man still must die, but it is a heroic confrontation. The poet, who sees dualism of man and spirit, will not proclaim a unity he cannot discover; but he maintains that man in his sphere can exemplify some of the nobility of the spiritual.

This belief, of course, is a reaffirmation. The poet is attempting to solve the problems he has raised by reasserting the power and worth of ecstatic communion with a spiritual reality superior to earth and man. The poet is to imitate the gods, not to embrace the world. Eberhart does not inherit this posture from his own countrymen. Emerson had taught Whitman and the Americans who followed him that even the glorified must keep a foot on the ground, that the American scholar should "embrace the common . . . explore and sit at the feet of the familiar, the low."

And *A Bravery of Earth* shows no influence from Eliot, Pound, Frost, or Williams; for Eberhart's associations, as has been noted, are with the English Romantic poets. His poem is Wordsworthian in some of its meditative and narrative passages and in its use of tags from Plato's idea of definite stages in man's spiritual development; but it is Blakean in the fire of some of its lyrics. It is Shelleyan in that its resolution, like that of "Ode to the

West Wind," is an apotheosis: not a god, the poet will be godlike
in his defiance. Yet his "bravery," after all, is of the earth—it is
the sun that fevers him—and his hope in the end is to understand
the drives and destinies of men through their actions. The ending
thus shows the direction, though not the realization, of the development Eberhart's esthetics would undergo. One need not
lessen his admiration for American accomplishment in order to
recognize that, for a poet of Eberhart's bent, the choice of the
English Romantic model was fortunate.

The shifting speculations, the sometimes evanescent moods
and tracings of ideas in the book-length poem, are accompanied
by marked shifts and uncertainties in style. The poem has occasional disastrously bad lines (line 12: "Rabbits dash beneath the
brush"). It has, too, such overexclamatory, Wordsworthian lines
as "But most, my favorite flower, joyous/ I brought, the wild
tigerlily!" Overwrought and exaggerated passages and pages
of prosaic writing indicate that the poet is not yet sure-handed.
A *Bravery of Earth* is not a great poem. But it has a fervor that
carries the reader along and that is supported by enough poetic
evidence to keep the whole from collapse. In *Collected Poems*,
Eberhart reprints three passages as separate poems: "This
Fevers Me," "O Wild Chaos!," and "The Bells of a Chinese
Temple".

II   *Held by Mystery*: Reading the Spirit

In *Reading the Spirit* (1936) Eberhart is still pondering the
change from youth to adulthood, the hard lesson that the simple
harmony youth envisions does not reign in mortal life, that the
world offers not unity but dualism and complexity. As always,
the spirit that inspires him with emotional fervor also drives him
to seek understanding. His search is not intellectual but esthetic.
The volume's thirty-one poems—of which sixteen reappear in
Collected Poems—include odes, lyrics, and versified speeches.
Their subjects include desire for a moment of vision, thoughts
during a visit to Wordsworth's lakes, confrontations with decay
and death, laments for loss of life and youth, recognition of
destiny, and relationships with one's fellow men. Although
American experience in the 1930's was traumatic and although
Eberhart in conversation takes the interest of most mentally
active men in political and social issues, little in the volume
deals with the social situation. Even "1934," despite its title, is a
poem about the self, not about the times. Eberhart, that is,

remains his own man; he is no more likely to be swept up by sociopolitical currents than by literary ones.

The man who speaks in these poems (surely Eberhart himself) knows that eventually he must accept this world and its ills, especially mortality. But, like Whitman in the opening sections of "When Lilacs Last in the Dooryard Bloom'd," Eberhart is not yet quite ready to welcome the realizations he already knows he must reach. Intellect and emotion both tell him that he must make hard recognitions, But he delays for a time full esthetic acceptance. Perhaps Eberhart was making a deliberate attempt to prolong his period of "second awareness," fearing that, if he gave in to knowledge, he might lose the creative tension that enabled him to write. Perhaps he felt also that to make a genuine acceptance he would have to have more experience, would have to probe further. Perhaps he even felt that, being still a young man, he had time enough to develop intellectual and emotional readiness. That one eventual resolution of his problems would be acceptance of a generalized Christianity is suggested by numerous allusions to God and Christ, just as his eventual recognition of the inextricable, if not always harmonious, unity of flesh and spirit is suggested in "Suite in Prison" and " 'In a Hard Intellectual Light.' "

But the typical resolution in this period is that of "1934"—the declaration that mystery holds him—and that of "The Ground-hog," the heightened, protesting lament about mortality; the postulating of reasons and reassurances would come later. Meanwhile, one step toward development of solutions is the pruning away of a variety of unsatisfactory answers. Therefore, one finds him dismissing in "Silence" the merely contemplative life; in "1934," rejecting mysticism (not the same at all as mystery); in "Cynic Song," attacking the bucolic; in "Maya and the Hunter," spurning the idea of living in fantasy. A poet who in youth was wonderstruck by perception of glory found all these possibilities tempting. At this stage, finally, Eberhart could still write fondly of "sun"—of the uncomplicated, awe-compelling glory of the universe that was sufficient to hold him in earlier years; and he could still ask " 'Where Are Those High and Haunting Skies?,' " though mind and feeling told him that, for resolutions, he must look to the earth.

A characteristic of Eberhart's work from the first to the latest is a fondness for words. If one accepts W. H. Auden's dictum that this penchant is the mark of poetic talent,[2] he may accept as evidence that Eberhart is talented the humorous "The Rape of the Cataract" and the several pieces in which his playfulness and his liking for paradox result in the creation of poems that are almost riddles. In "The Rape of the Cataract," Eberhart sustains some of the mock-heroic, high comic mood of Pope's "The Rape of the Lock." The poem draws on Eberhart's own experience in 1930 when he tutored two sons of the king of Siam while the king himself underwent surgery to remove a cataract.

The king was to be operated on at Johns Hopkins Hospital, but his retinue demanded that the entire hospital be turned over to him. The American doctor refused; the impasse was solved when the king's court was offered the Whitelaw Reid mansion in White Plains, New York. About a third of the mansion (the "palace" of the poem's fourth stanza) was rebuilt to serve as a royal surgery. When the cataract had been removed, the prime minister carried it past the whole court to demonstrate that the royal eye had been properly dealt with. The poem, which remarks about some of these circumstances, presents in an amused though respectful way some of the minor incidents of behavior that illumine differences between American and Siamese culture.

Riddlelike poems prove useful instruments for exploring some of the paradoxes of existence. The speaker in "Maze" begins like one expressing a young man's belief in harmony of man and nature:

> I have a tree in my arm,
> There are two hounds in my feet,
> The earth can do me no harm
> And the lake of my eyes is sweet.

But the poet then laments that the prettiness is gone, and he asks why the "will" has given him kingly visions of a happiness he cannot achieve. He blames man, who "imagined imagination" and "uncreated creation"—who, in becoming self-aware, in realizing as only human beings can that imagination is distinct from reality, broke up the harmony between being and nature. The speaker realizes that the blissful harmony he had imagined is not to be found. Knowing the good and evil of existence, he has lost his innocence. Though without specific theological allusions, the poem suggests parallels with the Garden of Eden story. Some passages are prosaic, but the Blake-like charm of the beginning gives a glow to the whole poem.

The relationship between man and force is explored in "Request for Offering," which envisions at the heart of the universe an implacable power, a "baleful lion" to whom man must offer innocence, a sacrifice that is both nourishing and sexual.[3] But, when innocence resists the lion's assault, he withdraws. The offering has appeased the rage of the implacable without actual sacrifice being necessary. Perhaps the poet intends an analogy with works of art, offerings which he sometimes speaks of, as in "1934," as superior to action and prayer.

Whatever understanding man develops, Eberhart even this early in his career sometimes feels that he must not only grudgingly admit but must also recognize and even welcome claims of the flesh. The speaker in "'In a Hard Intellectual Light'" at first declares that, following the light not of spirit but of intellect, he will quell all demands of the flesh and build a remote "citadel" that will be beautiful though not visible to man. It is as though the speaker would achieve a moment of perfect calm removed from all desires and passions of this world—a notion that seems to tempt Eberhart, since he often speculates upon it. The speaker declares that this fortress of intellect will inspire his spirit and close off the body's demands. From its elevation, he will have a vision of man's "moral grandeur," of a supranatural peace and purity. But the speaker cannot maintain for long that a man may escape from the necessities of his flesh. "Poverty" and "Death" bring him back to mortal concerns, to the world his flesh knows. Indeed the very intellect that enables him to plan to evade the necessities of mortal existence brings him back to the "truth" of that experience.

"'My Bones Flew Apart'" celebrates simplicity and unity, and it contrasts again what man imagines and reality. The striking idea of the title and opening line conveys the idea of multiplicity. When the speaker's bones scatter, he finds that, instead of the oblivion he had expected, he has entered a "vale of lamentation" dominated by the "bone God." He has desires and passions, at least for escape from mortality. He bemoans the fact that time goes on endlessly, but he changes; and he is disturbed because parts that he had thought dead take on new existence. The scene worsens: a cold mist rises, and the "bone God" sighs that the man is what intellect will bring him to—a fiction and a source of new experience and new tears. The speaker's spirit gasps; it is sunk in depression at the realization that his postmortal experience is no better than what he has known on earth. But the sun, Eberhart's favorite embodiment of spiritual inspiration, restores the speaker's shattered being to "knitted unison"; and he realizes that "truth is but simplicity," that reliance upon the intuition that a spiritual dimension exists in man is more rewarding than dependence on intellect. Now spiritually alive, he demonstrates virtue by offering his example to a neighbor still on earth. As in " 'In a Hard Intellectual Light' " Eberhart is telling his reader that intellect will lead him astray if, in his development of it, he neglects inspiration. The sort of jargon that a poet relying on intellect might produce is mocked in "The Return of Odysseus," a poem that fails because the reader does not know what is being lampooned by its ludicrous exaggerations of diction and figures.

As a meditative poet with an interest in spiritual awareness, Eberhart speculates often on the characteristics of moments of inspiration. These moments frequently are accompanied by a calm though not necessarily static quiet. "Caravan of Silence," written for J. L. Sweeney,[4] compares three kinds of quietness exemplified by travelers halted for the night on a Near Eastern desert. The first man, lulled by wine, passes an untroubled sleep without illusions but also without imagination. The second, who sits awake, could have some slight influence on the world about himself because he has desires that would to some extent change it. But his thinking is unimportant because it produces only self-centered rapture. The third man, a philosopher, is a man of vision who, seeing things as "they are," is indifferent to personal desire. He knows the eternity of sun and man, and because he has knowledge of reality he can affect the world. By his contemplations, he can make earth both "Colder and goldener"; through his vision, he can see to its depths and appreciate its beauties. The rhymed lines are worked in the tetrameter-with-variations that is one of Eberhart's favorite meters. Some wordings are plainly trite ("the gold ball" for the sun), and some are vague ("the vast of thoughts that sky him").

Artificiality of syntax and softness of language nearly ruin "Ode to Silence," which, despite its title, is more neo-Victorian than Miltonic or Keatsian in its content. The speaker appeals to Silence to help him still his grief at the death of a woman. For a time, he associates Silence with the dank and the bleak; and he then calls for soft music. But he returns to Silence—whose "dismal cave" he now sees as a "purple tunnel"—as the true quality of the universe's grandeur. Silence, offered in immaculate simplicity to the sun, will bring a "radiancy that casts no shade," the "Universal fire." The poem is wordy, afflicted with quasi-Romantic diction ("grot" for "grotto"; "whisper-shine" for a noon sun that bears a message) and forced syntax ("tarns of melancholy heights of hills"). The objection is not to the poet's experimenting but to his preservation of such a piece in *Collected Poems*.

"Four Lakes' Days" owes its Romantic-exclamatory view of the English Lake District to Wordsworth, though some of its quirks in expression are echoes of Gerard Manley Hopkins: "height/ Down-dooms"; "foot-increasing Esthwaite/ Water is, o the green! . . . " The opening exclaims over the region's delights for eye and mind, and the second and third sections find similar appeals even on a day of bleak rain and in hours spent hiking over hills made gloomy by dark waters and desolate pits. Though these sections do not have the exultation of some of Eberhart's lyrics, they sustain the air of delighted report. The final section, however, too easily uses the device of matching the experience of a storm on the hills to heroic defiance on the part of the speaker. One detects the poet strainnig for effect as he gives details in an excessively Latinate diction ("lambency," "Clamour clouds") and as he relies upon trite wording ("elemental passion," "terrible immediacy"). The poem gives the realization that sometimes "quiverness" (openness to strong feeling) may bring a "catharsis" that revitalizes after too much of men and cities.

A cry for the moment of rapture makes up " 'Where Are Those High and Haunting Skies?' " This title (the words are those of the opening line) is so compelling that one is surprised to find little else in the poem that is vivid. The poet laments the inaccessibility of those "skies," those inspired moments when he was beyond wind and desire. The world intrudes, narrowing his sight; the senses "bless and quell," give pleasure and calm his fevers; but the speaker will not supppress his yearning. He wishes for the "abrupt essence," the truth that comes by inspiration, and for the "final shield," the comprehension that saves man from defeat despite his mortality.

Two rather long poems come to two different resolutions of the poet's problem—his need for comprehension or, at least, release. The 144 lines of "Suite in Prison" move from bitter meditation upon the horrors of death and the grave to a litany-like prayer. The first section of the poem speaks of the grave's production of a "monstrous bloom," a numbness that gradually overtakes all remnants of feeling. The skeletons of lovers may have an extended wait for final death since "The earth is long at marrying the bone." But they feed new growth, "great regiment/ Of babes with petal spears. . . . " The speaker, realizing that he will himself be food for worms, expresses a grimly humorous defiance as he asks whether the worm can be aware of the knowledge of Plato and the idea of Christ contained in the brain it feeds on.

The second section, "Address to You," depicts the difficulties of attempting to find relief and comprehension by communion with another person. The poet cannot discern the "East," the genius or guiding spirit of another; he regrets that "we do not in Univerals sit," that we are material individuals instead of abstractions. The direction plainest to all men is West, the death which hungers to eat mankind. Letting another life come, perhaps through his love-making, man defeats Winter. The poet finally tells the person he addresses to leave because his brow remains "foreign." The one reality the speaker can be sure of is that his own eyes exist, that he himself has being.

The grave, though horrifying, appears to be not absolutely destructive; but answers to the questions that speculation raises are not to be found by efforts at communion with others. In the third section the poet relates his attempts to find answers by running abroad in nature. The sun seemed soothing to him, seemed to accompany him until he reached for it only to discover that "the sky was not grass," that it was not accessible to him. Alone again, he wept until "a flame," a renewed energy or vision, drove him on. He ran to the edge of night; a hand seemed to grab him; and he heard "a monstrous wailing" but discovered only emptiness. Distraught, he prayed for death.

The poet in the fourth section accepts the hard paradoxes of human existence. The very sunlight that inspires also incarcerates and damns; and knowledge of good and evil, of death, drives man to question and to despair. He must recognize that men are without hope, that they are created only to be destroyed because in their destruction they constitute praises of the "killing" power that governs them. Neither "Furies of action," those who strive against destiny, nor "Angels of solitude," the contemplative, can avoid mortality. A man must remember who and what he is because "Vision without memory has no portents," will not lead to accomplishment of his task. The speaker wills to identify with the future, "terrible and evil" though he expects it to be. Up to this point the poem has some of the energy of "The Groundhog" and "'I Walked out to the Graveyard to See the Dead'"; but, lacking the unifying central theme and the vividly concrete circumstances of such poems, it remains somewhat prosaic and inchoate.

Section V, "The Bath Room," however, is a presentation of a

man in a state of near hysteria, vivid enough to stand comparison
with Theodore Roethke's "The Lost Son." Eberhart's poem
couples exact details with fanciful inventions (shoes of polished
cowhide that "want their grass"); it leaps in eccentric but controlled gusto from the realistic to the mythological ("And I'll on
no pillow moan,/ Nor in the balefires fight"); it sets a mood
that enables the poet in two lines to allude without strain to
Khubla, Akhnaton, and "The Beast." The experience ends with
the poet's ironically declaring that, "in the middle/ Of this
doom," he will be neither unobservant nor superheroic nor stub-
born: he will simply name and refer to things as they are.

Things as they are include a table which is said to wear a
"white surplice" but later is described as an "albino crow":
it stands, perhaps, for an altar that is false and offers no
redemption. The ideas of religion and whiteness lead to the
final section's appeal to God to "stabilise," "qualify," and "admit"
the poet. His legs fail, his blood thins, his eyes lead him astray;
and his passions—pride, desire, love—are excessive. He prays to
"qualify"—to see pride put down, desire fulfilled, and love made
effective. If the Lord will "admit" him, he will rejoice despite
the suffering his knowledge brings him; contained in God's
"atmosphere," he will also be caught up in the "dancing" of
God's "ecstasy." If the fourth stanza of this final section consists
in part of inaccessible metaphor, the other six stanzas of the
section succeed because of their gusto. Occasional artificialities
of syntax (as in the third line of Stanza 3: "The rare air them
avails") work well because they help keep the otherwise fairly
prosaic expression from flatness. The chief conveyer of feeling,
however, is the litanylike rhythm, one Eberhart developed in
some of his later work.

The danger of surrendering all grasp on reality and the continuing paradox that the sun that inspires brings man a realization
of his powerlessness before universal forces are illustrated in
"The Transfer," a poem more unified than "Suite in Prison"
because it has a narrative thread of physical actions. As the poet
in spring watches an island of ice that is borne along in a river,
he thinks he sees in its gemlike, reflecting surface "the visionary
gleam" (the words, of course, are from Wordsworth's "Ode,"
line 56). Drawn to so enchanting a power, he leaps; and, exultant,
he slips "inside the ice." The world appears no more "as it is"
because the poet has merged with his vision; he has become
heroic and timeless. In his contemplation, he knows only the

"natal awareness of eternal harmony," and he declares that "Realisation of being is unchanging felicity."

But the reader will recall from "A Bravery of Earth" that the state of serene harmony is one known only by the immature. Even as the poet delights in his contemplative triumph, he feels a dread that deepens as the sun begins to break up the floe. The sunlight has inspired him, but it has also reawakened knowledge of reality, of harshly omnipotent force. Just as the ice the poet stands on starts over a dam, he grabs for a manlike tree on the riverbank and swings to safety. Association with the human, and with material nature, has saved one who was about to be drowned because he had let himself be drawn away from reality.

For Eberhart, vision can never become earthly reality because the truth that man dies always intrudes. "Necessity" gives the poet's meditations as he observes the courageous but doomed behavior of a woman dying of cancer. Nature, the reader is told, is using her as a "seed" for its own aims; and, though she maintains courage, her agony reveals itself in her lips and eyes. Man must accept the fact that there is no hope, that it is impossible for the woman to save herself by an act of will. The poet realizes that the woman's fate proves that men are without certainties and that even love offers no saving permanency. Like the passions that control man's being during an act of love, her dying proves that, at his most intense moments, man is subject to "a hid purpose" that overmasters his human will. Knowing her subjection, the woman is essentially alone. This aloneness gives her stature; for, says the poet, the highest qualities of spirit are expressed in shunning desire for safety, in asking fate to bite even more deeply. In such "nobility" one attains heights, an "Unutterable remoteness" and "Intolerable nearness" that bring a full realization of the "separateness," the necessary loneliness of each man.

Observing bodies of animals gives rise to two fine poems. "For a Lamb" is a successful lyric that muses about the nature of death. In eight lines it gives the realistic scene of decay, raises poignant questions, and concludes that understanding of the matter can only be to "Say he's in the wind somewhere,/ Say, there's a lamb in the daisies." The poet cannot be accused of prettifying the decay, for in the first line he describes the lamb as "putrid," and in the fourth line he says that "the guts were out for crows to eat." Of a chemical immortality Eberhart can be sure; beyond that, his statement in this poem does not go. Yet the tone is appealingly melancholic, rather than despairing.

One senses that the poet has hope, whether he can find logical grounds for it or not.

Eberhart presents his most deeply moving recognition of the universality of death in "The Groundhog." From the beginning, the emphasis is not on the animal itself but on the poet's reaction to it:

> In June, amid the golden fields,
> I saw a groundhog lying dead.
> Dead lay he; my senses shook,
> And mind outshot our naked frailty.

The almost laconic report in the first two lines, heightened by the adjective "golden" and the unobtrusive rhythm, is made emotionally meaningful by the inversion of structure of "Dead lay he" in the third line. Having immediately "outshot our naked frailty," gone beyond recognition of physical death to think of causes and meanings, the poet next noted that the animal's form "began its senseless change" in the summer, the season when life is at its height. He reacted "Half with loathing, half with a strange love," with revulsion tempered by the recognition that what the animal's body was undergoing is the destiny of all living things. Poking at the body with a stick resulted in a fever of energy on the part of the maggots, a fever representing an immense "Vigour" comparable to, perhaps actually produced by, the sun. The creature's decay was the work of ultimate natural force; but the poet, in contrast, was victim of a "sunless trembling": his reactions were those of a living creature seeing, and dreading, his own destiny. His thrust with the stick had done neither good nor harm, for human intervention is powerless. Though looking straightforwardly at the most horrifying aspect of death, the poet kept his "reverence for knowledge," his belief that the process of decay must have a meaning beyond its chemistry. He went on his knees to pray "for joy in the sight of decay"; but, when no revelation came, he left the scene.

Returning in the autumn, he was still willing to confront the body without turning away. But the autumn proved to be a season of the spirit as well as of the year: he found himself "in intellectual chains," without emotional response. The meaning, the reader is told, lay in the "year"; and it rose and subsided with the energy of nature. Though at the moment he was in a different season of existence, the poet was as much in the grip of natural energies as the groundhog. In the next summer he "chanced" upon the sight again. Now there was nothing but a little hair and bones; and, though he found the skeleton "Beautiful as architecture," he did not see it as an imaginative being aware of significances. Lines 41 and 42 tell of a fourth visit: "It has been three years, now./ There is no sign of the groundhog." Realization of ultimate disappearance brought a climactic access of feeling:

> I stood there in the whirling summer,
> My hand capped a withered heart,
> And thought of China and of Greece,
> Of Alexander in his tent;
> Of Montaigne in his tower,
> Of Saint Theresa in her wild lament.

With the animal's body gone, the poet could react to the aware-ness—most profound in the summer season of full experience, of full light—that not only the groundhog but also man's empires and leaders must disappear. The ending has been criticized as an evasion of the issues the poem raises and as a merely declam-atory peroration.[5] But it certainly is appropriate if one sees that, from the beginning, the focus is on the poet's sight of the body—not on the body's decay.

The poem's success arises from Eberhart's insistence on recog-nizing both spirit and flesh. It presents the reactions of a sensitive man fascinated by observation of an inevitable process. The dramatic tension is high because his effort to find relief for his horror results only in realization of the frailty of all living beings and of all that man creates. Eberhart allows interplay of per-ception and emotion to build the poem without imposition of solutions to its problems. The poem is artful in its tactics as well as in its strategy. For example, the names in the ending lines—of a conqueror, a sage, and a saint—are chosen to give a range of possibilities. The lines are tied together by careful alliteration. In the first four lines, quoted above, are such pairings and repetitions as "golden," "groundhog"; "senses," "shook," "shot"; 'out-," "our"; "lying," "lay"; "dead," "Dead." The paralleling of emotional experience to seasons of the year is an effective use of convention, as is the occasional contrast of the poet's responses with the nature of the season. The poem brings together Eber-hart's favorite themes—the theme of light and vision, and one of mortality. The result is a major presentation of Eberhart's early response to realization of death, the mood of questioning, lamenting protest. Perhaps the most often anthologized of his poems, 'The Groundhog" is also one by which Eberhart chooses to measure his accomplishment.[6]

Where Eberhart understood himself to be in the mid-1930's he

shows in "1934," a poem that in direct, careful first-person statement seems explicitly, and rather movingly, autobiographical.
As the horns blare for New Year's Eve, the speaker, a poet, takes
stock of his esthetic development. The mock-heroic beginning
gives the note of subtle humor proper not only to so grand a
project but also to personal assessment at the age of thirty. The
speaker is not sure what stance he should adopt toward the
world, but he knows that intellect cannot answer his questions.
He has taken a step toward discovery by traveling in the imagination; but he has not followed the path of mysticism; indeed,
he is "ashamed" of self-centeredness and finds himself spitting
upon "all worlds of Spain," perhaps thinking of Spain as the
home of such mystics as Saint John of the Cross and Teresa of
Avila. Passage of time, meanwhile, lessens the ardor of his search.
Knowing that both action and prayer are futile, he determines
to find answers to man's despair through poetry. Putting reality
and fiction together, he has found strength and compassion, while
continuing to recognize that "And ever and still the weight of
mystery/ Arrows a way between my words and me."

The fifteen poems in *Reading the Spirit* that are not reprinted
in *Collected Poems* are not below average in quality. Reviewing
them strengthens the impression that Eberhart at this stage
recognized what he terms necessity but was not reconciled to it;
he was still meditating, questioning, lamenting, and protesting
the destiny he refused to overlook or evade. "'World's Mere
Environment'" contrasts time, the permanency in the universe,
with environment, the world one finds himself in. World is
mortal like man himself, rather than wondrous and spiritually
reasoning. Awkward syntax is functional because it contributes
an appropriate sense of playfulness, but similar awkwardness in
"Cynic Song" seems to result only from uncertainty of attitude.
The poet celebrates in the first six lines his son who has yet to be
born (Eberhart, indeed, did not marry until five years after
Reading the Spirit was first published). The ending two lines
are reminiscent in mood of Blake's "Little Black Boy"—"And I'll
his child hands warm/ And feed him on thought tenderly"—but
their rhythm is out of joint with the slower, somewhat tortured
pace of the earlier lines. The indication of cynicism in the title
suggests that the poet knows that such bucolic delight as that
he anticipates is a sentiment of fantasy, not a quality of relationships among living beings.

Instead of the bucolic, a sensitive man may experience the
moment of "chill calm beyond despair" presented in "'In the

Evening Stark and Bare.' " This brief mood piece is effective in
its quiet simplicity. Except for a slight rhythmic weakness in the
opening stanza, and the somewhat trite expression of the fourth
line ("Silence was sounding . . ."), the poem, in Eberhart's
mature manner, skillfully mingles the concrete, the musical, and
the abstract.

The certainty of destiny is suggested in both "Fragments" and
"Maya and the Hunter." In "Fragments," a monologue, the
speaker, comparing men to the fragments of past civilizations,
reflects that men too will leave only remnants. Death and decay
are demanded neither by fellow men nor by an ideal of beauty,
but by "the sunned earth." Men are, it would seem, creatures
not of imagination nor of an abstraction but of the cosmos, the
sun that governs men's world for purposes hidden from them.
The self-consciousness men win by "daring" only deepens the
"hurt" in them because it shows them their end. The poem ends
conventionally, with the speaker directing his lover to come with
him because only they, the earth they are part of, and the love
that links them are real. By implication, talk of other ideals, of
heroisms and immortality, is all ultimately unreal.

"Maya and the Hunter" extends Eberhart's picture of the
unreal. Maya, a goddess totally sure of herself, showers "her
Western cities" with material goods produced by "soot-faced"
workers who adore her gratefully. The name Maya is appropriate,
for Hinduism uses it for what it sees as the mistaken notion that
the world is made up of diversity rather than unity—the ignorance
that prevents man from realizing his own identity with the
spiritual. In Eberhart's poem, Maya has erred in assuming that
giving "gauds" to her people will make them wise. In the second
stanza, she develops doubts, finding that not the material progress
of her people but only the sun can soothe her. The third stanza
brings, in "the Hunter," a character perhaps analogous to Orion,
who in myth is a lustful giant.

In this poem, the Hunter is a scientist, a devotee of measure-
ment who fatuously thinks that, by his instruments, he can
understand the world. When Maya and the Hunter copulate,
one supposes that they might give birth to "a master boy"; for
insufficient by themselves, Maya and "the Hunter" together could
be capable of producing a being of ultimate grandeur and force.
The poem ends with a twenty-seven-line stanza which, as frequently in Eberhart's work ("The Groundhog"), comes at the
poem's central problem from a new tangent. The lines are given
as the thoughts of a speaker, probably Maya herself, who recalls

her time in the womb, a period of complete security with all desire satisfied. This bliss, of course, supported only a totally false view of existence: "I imagined, and revolved around/ The flying point at the unreal North." The speaker, when in the womb, necessarily formed ideas only in imagination, had thoughts oriented to an impossible pole. The ending serves not as a continuation—the argument, so to speak, is finished at the end of the fourth stanza—but as an indirect reiteration of the point that to live in fantasy is to limit oneself to unreality.

Another visionary moment is the experience of "Beyond Son Rapiña." In the first two stanzas, Eberhart praises white mountains that look like "Clean death." They are shaped by his perception of them and seem identical with the impersonal, hard but bright "knowledge" he acquires in an inspired instant. But the moments of vision do not last. The speaker, who returns to the peace of the valley, comments that the trees he finds there are creatures of "Necessity," tortured in shape; but they continue to offer fresh leaves to the sun. In lines that might have been turned out by a fumbling Yeats, Eberhart ends the poem with a salute to the trees as resembling human beings: "O leafy eyes! (O marble sky!)/ From the body's symbol bole." Such praise of the ability to survive is not common in Eberhart's work, which is more likely to emphasize the certainty of fate. The two Spanish words in the title are a place name; in English, the title would read approximately "Beyond the Sound [of] Violence," a meaning Eberhart presumably was aware of.

Two love poems—the one fairly successful, the other a failure —indicate something of Eberhart's abilities at this period. "If This Be Love" maintains the heightened mood set by its first two lines' skillful combination of the concrete and the abstract: "If this be love, then let me leap/ Into the abstract austerity, . . ." The poet speaker urges the lover, perhaps himself, to "Contaminate" the innocent to bring her wisdom. A figure vivifies the situation: "And a cone of love around the honey/ Comes; but the bee cuts there." The lover sees the paradox that the cruelty necessary to teach reality is kind because it achieves its purpose. Yet he can bemoan the loss that knowledge of reality will bring.

In " 'You, Too, Are Coming up,' " a lover addresses Maia—a name evoking the memory of the Classical mountain nymph because the speaker is one who has climbed to "rare air."[7] As he sees Maia coming to join him, he remarks on the decline of their former love. He prefers that they renounce any efforts at renewal of love, for such efforts might bring them back to reality, might

destroy the "crystal vision" that they had sustained out of desire
for each other when separate. The poem has too many prosaic
lines—the first four—to achieve vividness; and its motion is sometimes interrupted because it lacks a controlling rhythm.

In "New Year's Eve," the speaker muses on the analogy of the
moment between years to his relationship with a woman. As he
talks, he realizes that, in their moment of entrancement, they
both are unwilling to face the light that they know to be the
truth. But truth prevails: the speaker recognizes that even the
sun must eventually die, that men and mountains and all ·the
flora and fauna of the earth share a common "heart" and "mind,"
a common destiny. Joined in love, the man and woman can
represent this "universal unity" that they do not dare to confront
intellectually, the unity that is "timeless" and "out of space."
The concept of a transcendental mind and spirit that fills all
matter as well as all life is not one Eberhart develops extensively,
and he omitted this poem from *Collected Poems.*

The problem of unity, as exemplified in the relationship of
two lovers, is explored at greater length in "Dissertation by
Wax Light," a poem of six sections of three to seven stanzas each.
The first two sections meditate on the self as the chief problem
in love. Seeing how two lovers remain apart, each using the
other but unwilling to surrender his own ego, the poet speculates
that such separating individualism can end only when love finds
a harbor in God. Eberhart will not remain satisfied with such
ethereal speculation, however; for in Section II, he continues
that the self is the "bane" of love, that the solidity of love is not
provable by rational methods. Love, he decides, "is but warm
simplicity," is a quality of human relationships rather than a
spark of divinity. Both the syntax and the metaphor of the last
two stanzas of Section II are puzzling, not because of complexity
in the conception behind them, but because the poet's cleverness
seems to have overcome his directness.

Having decided—like Robert Frost in "Birches"—that earth
is the right place for love, Eberhart in sections III and IV
contrasts a purely intellectual and a purely rhapsodic love. The
one affair, a courtship by correspondence, is a verbalized relationship which, since words substitute for sexual activity, the poet
punningly styles a "literal copulation." All the while, the "taper,"
the fire of passion, threatens to break through. Section IV presents
the sharply differing experience of love under an Italian sun
where one needs "only to be alive" to exist in a harmony of joy
that convinces him that everything else, all intellectualization,

is only an illusion. But Section V corrects this view, for the idyllic is also out of touch with the truth of human experience. All dogma must be eliminated, or the "City"—apparently a truly perceptive love, a state somewhat analogous to the idea of a City of God—will be only a sepulchral monastery tower in which a mad monk, ignorant of the drive toward love that quivers his flesh, dances out a wasted life. These speculations too fail to satisfy the urges that drive the poet. In the last section, he notes the bees that work outside his window and recalls how he and his lady had brought gold to the dun hillside. Fretfully, he kills a spider; and, awakened by this act of irritation, he smells the brimstone, senses the fear of mortality. He concludes that "Hope can make its pure moan"—a fine ending that indicates both the existence of hope and the harsh stringencies that restrain it.

Eberhart's ability to make poetry out of materials that in prose description seem to be in bad taste, if not outright horrifying, is well exemplified in "Meditation on the Sun" and in "Job." In "Meditation on the Sun," the speaker imagines himself a philosopher-worm consuming the body of the sun in his search for wisdom. The monologue is paced to give the effect of hard, careful thinking, with rather abrupt turns in thought suited to the fevered hurry. The philosopher-worm hopes to ease his sense of mortality, recalls the sacrifices he has made to keep his life, but realizes in the end that he can never by his own efforts obtain the answers and pleads that the inspiration whose body he ravages will "fool time,/ But fool not me," that it will hold off the death that time would bring him and be revelatory rather than concealing. The poem is successful because its pitch and pace, its diction and imagery, are convincingly appropriate expressions of its argument. The conception of one burrowing in a corpse is startling, but the emphasis upon colors and atmosphere give the poem a prettiness that saves it from morbidity. "Job" is a harsh eight-line poem depicting a bestial victim of disease and torture. Disgust is held off by rhythm and by the romantically pretty fifth line ("In the half-way murk and sad kingdom of pain").

In "Meditation on the Sun" and "Job," Eberhart's imagination, limited to defined circumstances, produces moving poems. An unsuccessful piece having considerable realistic detail but lacking firm control of circumstance is "On First Hearing Beethoven's Opus 127, at 23 Fitzroy Square." An attempt to match in language the emotions the speaker purportedly felt upon hearing music, the poem fails because it resorts to exclamation that seems closer

to rant than to esthetic response. One can be suspicious of music
appreciation set down in lines like these:

> But Rejoice! it is a boon, a red flare,
> Suddenly the world is dry, clear as a bell.
> I am a fountain pen with the cap burst off,
> O the world is all blue! blue! blue!

In rhetorical form, the poem is clever; for the poet intermixes
short and relatively long passages and brings the poem to a
properly abrupt ending. But exterior form cannot make up for
the lack of inner coherence, of a controlling metaphor and attitude
that would give precision to the language.

How much more deeply Eberhart is moved by the theme of
mortality than by that of hope—probably because he believes
mortality to represent the truth—is apparent in the contrast
between "'Death Is Indescribably Much on Me'" and "Song
of the Soul." The first poem begins with three stanzas of detail
to support its opening assertion, detail which includes metaphor
and description, a scene in a crypt, and an afternoon's vision.
"Hope, Passion, Desire, Fame, Defeat" are described as "hollow"
because Death is the only reality, the one in which the Love
that entrances man during life will end. Recalling a death in
Minnesota and again asserting his entrapment, the speaker concludes with a hope for final recognition and fruition, apparently
for understanding. This hope is eventually to be surpassed also
by "the silence of death." Though not one of Eberhart's more
moving poems, it is moderately successful because it grounds
its assertions in detail, observed or imagined, that is sufficient
to provide support for them. That "Song of the Soul" is unsuccessful may be owing to the fact that the optimism Eberhart purports to express in it is a quality for which he frequently finds
no support. The poem turns to excessive repetition of words and
sounds and to flat "poetic" lines ("Of men and women and girls
and boys, of gods"), even to Kiplingesque moralizing ("And
Purpose rides the days nights Will the foaming years").

III   *Preparing Resolutions*: Song and Idea

Resolutions are still held in abeyance in *Song and Idea* (1942).
There are continued presentiments that solutions will come
through limited acceptance of religion and, principally, through
avowal of the flesh; but full acknowledgment is not yet made.
The forty-one poems, of which twenty-six are reprinted in *Collected Poems,* express desire for unity, discovery of beauty in

corruption, the rapture of moments of visionary understanding, and the effects of the contrast between the poet's sense of wonder and his mature knowledge. There are, however, two additions to the elements which eventually constitute the solution of Eberhart's problem. One is the idea of love, an energy that at this point Eberhart usually mentions only as a vaguely cosmic force though occasionally he finds it exemplified in human relationships. More important is an increasing sense of assurance that death is not extinction. The strongest source for belief in immortality is the poet's sense of communion with his dead parents, a sense brought by memory and by association with places that seem to put him in touch with a universal spirit.

"Orchard," an apparently autobiographical poem, tells the reader that the "strong right of human love" is a challenge to mortality. Sharing a moment of quiet but strong feeling, each member of a family is aware that the mother is "stalked/ By the stark shape of malignant disease." The father has the practicality to recognize the fact of death but the spirit to remain courageous. The mother herself pours forth a love "divinely magnified" by "imminent despair." The three children are only half aware of the seriousness of her illness. The poet recalls years later the moment as one that exemplifies endurance of life's circumstances by those who recognize mortal fate but are fortified by strength of spirit. "Orchard" reports adjectivally, rather than by means of imagery derived from vivid perception. The second stanza is almost prose:

> Strongest was the father, of solid years,
> Who set his jaw against the coming winter,
> Pure, hard, strong, and infinitely gentle
> For the worst that evil brings can only kill us.

The lines are heightened, however, by the situation that is their context and by the fourth line's near aphorism that establishes a properly ironic yet sympathetic attitude.

More than a challenge, "At Night" is an assurance that the living can achieve emotional union with those now dead. The poet, meditating on the beach, finds that "still I do not understand," that he has no intellectual comprehension of why his parents have died. But love seems to flow over him, a love that intimates the presence of the parents his mind knows are dust. By the "sovereign" sea—perhaps a metaphor for faith—he is "rich with gifts"; for he senses his parents' "terrene presences": they seem alive not only in spirit but almost in flesh as well. The short poem's straightforward declarations and questioning, put in blank verse that is simple in syntax, make for a clarity that gives persuasive restraint to its almost incantatory presentation of wonderment. This wonderment gives Eberhart an assurance more profound than logic could provide.

"Orchard" gives a moderately heightened report of experience. "At Night" expresses an emotion that is deeper but still disciplined by the poet's sense of reality. In the seventy-one-line poem "The Soul Longs to Return Whence It Came," vision overpowers circumstance to produce high intensity. The poem moves from the almost laconic statement of its first seventeen lines to presentation of ardent emotional experience which ends in return to control by mind, but a control informed by new wisdom. Visiting the grave of his mother, the poet notes the roots that pierce it and thinks of all the world's dead. This reflection is too generalized to arouse intense emotion. But when dry leaves begin to rustle under the "motionless and brittle" sun—intimating, perhaps, an energy within the apparently dead—his "blood" begins to rise, and "I," the mind, is at last "out of command."

By line 45 the poet has become a "being of feeling alone." In this seizure, he flings himself on the earth and weeps in "pagan adoration," feeling "the actual earth of her." By line 51 he has himself become "Victor and victim of humility." Earlier in the poem, humility was a quality rising from all human loss, but now it has become personal. The experience ends in a moment of transcendence, a "wordless ecstasy" "Of mystery: where there is no thought/ But feeling lost in itself forever,/ Profound, remote, immediate, and calm." The moment passes; suddenly worried that he will look foolish, the poet steps away. Reason replaces ecstasy, but "blood" has given him new knowledge and he goes away from the graveyard "elated," saying "Mother, Great Being, O source of Life/ To whom in wisdom we return/ Accept this humble servant evermore."

The poem associates through its imagery the physical circumstances with each step in the journey toward new realization. For instance, in line 13, the "Little wind that frisked" is only a detail in a description of a fall day; but in line 33 this wind starts the rustling that inaugurates the change from mind to emotion. In turn, by line 57, the rustling has become a momentarily ominous sound produced by a seemingly sensate nature. This imagery also supports the progression which takes the poet from thought of his own mother to recognition of the pagan but convincing appeal of "Mother, Great Being," a god within nature.

In "The Soul Longs to Return Whence It Came," the poet

becomes humble as a man gifted with new understanding of universal power, a "pagan" strength which is both natural and spiritual. In "The Groundhog," Eberhart emphasizes the powerlessness of man as one subject to universal natural force; but in "Orchard," he stresses the moral right of frail man to endure as though he would prevail despite the sure approach of death. In "At Night" and "The Soul Longs to Return Whence It Came," he achieves actual communion with beings who are outside mortal life. He subsequently attains what is for him convincing emotional assurance that human immortality is possible.

At times, Eberhart has as speaker in a poem a character who talks from the grave or beyond. This device has been most notably exploited in American poetry of this century by Edgar Lee Masters and Edwin Arlington Robinson. But Masters and Robinson were using it for social criticism, as a means for revealing what they saw as the ugliness of small-town life. Eberhart's intentions are to explore death itself, its circumstances and significances. In "The Scarf of June," the speaker, being dead, is imprisoned in a winter far from the spring that is coming to earth. His physical elements—the roots he nourishes, his heart that now decays—may respond (through chemical process) to the season's urging, "But I, insensible to this,/ Will like a cold stone be." The "I," the true self of the speaker, is impervious to time, is one with "earth's inner being."

Death itself is the speaker in "Experience Evoked," a twenty-line address urging mankind to come to the ultimate state in which there will be a "harsh shroud over all." The first five lines make two allusions to Christian symbolism: a fir is presumably a Christmas tree; the "old Rose" to be sown is perhaps love of the Virgin. Men are urged to come from the "garden," the cemetery where their bodies decayed; special urging is directed to those who "grew tall" by defying the doom they knew would come. Although the poem's last five lines may be intended only to give the reader the choice of to "cry"—to celebrate—both those who died in infancy and those who died in age, the previous Christian allusions suggest that the reader is to regard the "babe bound" as the Christchild. The options thus are to celebrate either Christ or an old man representing one who lived in appreciation of nature. In any case, the final plea for the "harsh shroud" is a request for ultimate destiny. Whether this destiny is simple extinction or some other fate Eberhart does not say.

In "Two Loves," death makes complex a man's relationships to women, one of whom is dead, the other still alive. The man understands the influence of the living woman, but the persistence of his love for the woman now dead troubles him. He concludes that she was one who represented a "mood" that "had a right to die." The living girl who is his "passion," and who revives in him thoughts of the dead woman, seems indeed to "Come from the dead," to represent her spirit. The dead man who spoke in "The Scarf of June" contrasted his situation in spring with that of the living; the living man in "Two Loves" is puzzled by the resemblance of one living to one dead. There is a suggestion in these pairings of unity, whether by contrast or by comparison.

In "Burden" and in "'In Prisons of Established Craze,'" the motivation for the verse is Eberhart's continuing sense of the "unknown in knowing." As a comment on how a man living near a mountain finds that its snows load his heart, "Burden" somewhat resembles poetry by Robert Frost (as Eberhart observed in an interview).[8] But the inversion of line 4 ("... And never the sea") is in Eberhart's style, not Frost's; and the poem has a Romantic-declarative mood, an exuberance of assertion that is not typical of Frost's reflective caution. The man of "Burden" knows, by feeling rather than by intellect, that nothing can ease the burden of his heart, that he must forever scramble to conquer the mountain. One senses that the mountain represents knowledge, perhaps of mortality.

But though knowledge limits joy, it does not produce despair. "'In Prisons of Established Craze'" has most men, the sane, living in what are prisons and unable by any expression to break through the walls that surround them. Men must, therefore, accept time, revere the "silence" which is the only message destiny gives them. They must accept too the fact of the "senseless dissonance" between their cities, their community lives, and the green earth. Yet, despite the inability of men even to breathe harmoniously, there is somehow a "rhythm" to their existence. There is in the mind a "gauge," a check that stays them from suicide. The existence of this check suggests that there is reason to cling to life, even that there is a power superior to men that wills their living out their lifespan.

In several poems Eberhart explores relationships between joy, innocence, inspiration, and painful adult realizations. In "'When Doris Danced,'" the sun that in the first stanza is attracted to Doris is in the second stanza an enticer that leads her to lie with a man. The second stanza's irony—not a typical device for Eberhart—is strong enough to give a tone almost of anger, suggesting that Eberhart could have written effectively in this mood more often if he had been moved to do so. It also suggests that the poet is attracted to the innocence portrayed in the first stanza and saddened by the realism expressed in the second. One recognizes the similarity to Eberhart's own reluctant turn from the naïveté of sun to the dark knowledge of maturity.

"'Now Is the Air Made of Chiming Balls'" shows Eberhart still capable of presenting a simple moment of sheer delight. The striking picture of the title (used also as the first line) is reinforced by a selection of details from nature, which would be merely sentimental if it were not for the opening imagery. "Recollection of Childhood" is written with a child's eye for "the natural world of happy forms." The poem is reminiscent of some of Blake's "Songs of Innocence," but the touches of philosophy in lines 12, 15, and 16 are distinctively Eberhart's: he says that he will continue to desire and to act, to live in "melodious love" and, through these means, will touch "the very god of love." These assertions are in keeping with the innocence of the speaker.

But, of course, what Eberhart sees as adult awareness tells him that innocence does not reign in the world man knows. In "'If I Could Only Live at the Pitch that Is Near Madness,'" the speaker recognizes, sadly, that one cannot live at the height of sensory joy, in a fantasy of unlimited possibility. A child becomes a man, drawn along by time which passes like the hands of a clock, hands to which he seems to be bound. Nature, too, turns out to exist in time. And one's fellow men demand not expression of innocent delight but a "moral answer" to the philosophical and esthetic problem posed by mortality. Confronting this problem brings the death of the "I," the ego which a young man indulges. As an adult, he sees a world of complexity where only "necessity" is possible; and "truth," instead of gloating in childlike delight, laments like a bloodied infant. One recalls that Eberhart told his Modern Language Association audience that this poem was his escape from the depression of the 1930's. One may consider it to be, perhaps, not so much an escape as a recognition, a lament which is also an acceptance. But in most of this poem, as in "Recollection of Childhood" and in "'Now Is the Air Made of Chiming Balls,'" Eberhart expresses with simplicity and strikingly original imagery his sense of wonder.

Lament for the loss of innocence and wonder is the theme of "'The Full of Joy Do not Know; They Need Not.'" The first stanza states that the joyful, having "the light of Heaven," neither have nor need knowledge; they do not know even that life has disharmonies. The second stanza says that those who suffer see the truth. Knowing death, these are wise and, consequently, are hurt. If the first stanza in saying "let them have it" is faintly mocking the joyful for their ignorance, the second in speaking of "calculation" is faintly criticizing the knowledgeable.

Those too young to see meanings in death may of course experience it. "The Child" is an eight-line comment, almost a cry, giving the poet's observation of a five-year-old drawn to the edge of a cliff by the ocean. Though the Atlantic is summery, the poet remembers only the terror of the experience. The story is not concluded: the poem dwells rather on the feelings the incident aroused, reporting these as the poet experienced them though using a touch of childlike exclamation to make the situation graphic. There is a "fearful" cliff, the sapling on it that either tempts or perhaps offers a slight chance of safety, a dove "that will hurt me"—the child himself, who by his fall will horrify the observer, or perhaps a bird symbolizing a peace that is shattered. Over all the scene, there is the skyborne sense of destiny.

Though Eberhart adheres to professional standards in literary scholarship, he occasionally adopts the Romantic convention of ridiculing literary critics as rationalists or escapists—as men not attuned to a poet's sensitivities. "'The Critic with His Pained Eye'" is an assertion that the poet's sources are not accessible to the critic, that to perceive these sources the critic would have to be transformed. If the critic would be free—from rationalistic or other misconceptions—he would "love" instead of lie, would perhaps have empathy with the poet instead of applying logic to the nonlogical.[9] "'I Went to See Irving Babbitt'" mocks the Harvard humanist critic as a man who spoke only a Yankee-accented French that seemed forced beside the "nubian Swahili" the speaker of the poem says is his own tongue, a comparison perhaps intended to convey to us that Eberhart's American English seemed barbarous to Babbitt. Additional fun is the sight of Babbitt, "the hater of mechanical America," driving off in a Ford. The poem ends with mockery of Harvard, the archetypical American academy, first with a sing-song line, then with pseudo-Tennysonian onomatopoeia, next with a pun on the assumption that the university sets standards, and finally with a contrast between Shakespeare as described in Milton's "L'Allegro" (one who would "Warble his native wood-notes mild") and the scholar who warbles only footnotes.

Given the knowledge of mortality and the fact that man cannot

explain it, man may turn to meditation. The poems "The Humanist," " 'Man's Greed and Envy Are So Great,' " " 'The Goal of
Intellectual Man,' " and " 'I Walked out to the Graveyard to See
the Dead' " recommend meditation and consider some of the
answers it might lead to. Dismissing learning and physical action
as paths to comprehension, "The Humanist" argues that final
understanding comes only with acceptance of mystery. Because
men cannot arrive at answers to ultimate questions, they are
"Neither true nor free/ But truly human." What ultimate answers
may be is suggested by allusion to divinity: the mystery in which
man lives is said to be "Of God." The poem's emphasis, however,
is not on theology but on man. " 'Man's Greed and Envy Are so
Great' " also decries competition and action, saying that praise
properly goes to "Philosophic men." Again there is allusion to
divinity, this time to Christ; but, as in "The Humanist," emphasis
is upon man.

Eberhart pays the reverence of a nod in the direction of God
and Christ; but, when he chooses to become fairly explicit about
the solution to a problem, it is usually "love" that he advocates.
" 'The Goal of Intellectual Man' " advocates both the love and
the acceptance of this earth that become major components of
the answers Eberhart later develops for his problems. The poem
identifies the true intellectual not as the rationalist but as the
seeker of inspiration. What this seeker comes to will be neither
a mystic's merging with a universal, nor a barren extinction, but
a "Concrete, specific" human love—one exemplified on this earth
in the midst of the usual human difficulties and dangers. In a
letter telling about reading this poem at Brandeis University's
inauguration of a new president, Eberhart says: "I told them
that the poem held that there is more to life than intellect."[10]

Emphasis on the need to look for answers within the world
of human experience comes in " 'I Walked out to the Graveyard
to See the Dead.' " Finding that he cannot visit the cemetery
because the gates are locked, the poet turns to address a golden
pheasant which he sees seated on nearby boughs. The bird
looks "with fearful method," systematically and in some dread,
perhaps because the sunset will dim its colors. The poet tells
the bird not to wink at him, not to suggest a relationship. For
the poet, it seems, the bird symbolizes the magical, the unattainable, a beauty that may be attractive but is without meaning
for men. He consigns it to "the rafters of Montaigne."

Here, as in the ending of "The Groundhog," Montaigne seems
to be seen as a figure in a tower, as one remote from common

experience. To talk with "the Absolute," to speak of unearthly ideals, is to waste energy, as is concentration on the self. Like the golden bird, philosophical idealism and mysticism attract Eberhart's eye; but, at least when he wrote this poem, he would not be seduced away from the world. He is sure that "action," what a man must do, is to be learned only from "love of man." One may contrast this poem with "The Soul Longs to Return Whence It Came," in which the poet finds the cemetery unlocked and, entering, experiences a reassuring ecstasy. That Eberhart could write both poems shows that, in his search for answers, he could see more than one possible decision.

Eberhart's answer ultimately would be not to reject either vision or realism but to find the one within the other. But he has always been able to find realizations in brief moments of intense feeling. Such moments are often brought to him by observations of particulars associated with mortality, as in the many poems that recall experiences associated with the death of his mother. Among other poems telling of strong feeling aroused by details of mortality are " 'Let the Tight Lizard on the Wall,' " "The Largess," " 'When Golden Flies upon My Carcass Come,' " and "The Virgin." " 'Let the Tight Lizard on the Wall' " is told in a style close to that of Eberhart's riddle poems; it is appropriate because it helps suggest the speaker's disturbed state. Seeing a lizard on a wall, he apparently tickles it, then imagines sighting it in a gun (one rare meaning for 'Pipped" in line 6). He thinks of the creature when shot as exhaling its breath, an exquisite spirit whose departure represents the end of life, "time's fail." He thinks next of the lizard's decaying, though still fixed to the wall in defiance of the "canker pelts," the corrupting agents that attack it. Even in decay, the lizard has entered into a "marriage of the sky," has preserved an aura of beauty. The speaker nevertheless directs the creature to communicate no joy, for the world is "too delicate," too artificial to accept such a message. In the Blakean last stanza, the speaker exclaims over the "shimmer," the "protection," which the creature seems to symbolize.

A discarded cicada husk in "The Largess" represents to the poem's speaker an object of fear, a premonition of death's search for him; and he hopes that there is no analogy between his glances at the husk and death's anticipatory speculations on him: may death, he hopes, look rather at itself. As usual for Eberhart, however, the object giving rise to these speculations has a "wondrous lure," a beauty that attracts the speaker to examine it. He hopes that its form will somehow prove to differ from that it had when living; for a difference, one deduces, would suggest hope that the death represented by the husk was outlandish rather than expected. He supposes that memory of the husk will remain with him, and he directs the cicada itself to sing to him. But, though he is able to observe the husk, he can find no "sign" in it. He exclaims over the "eternal" it seems to suggest and pleads for a word it will not give him.

Even in thinking of his own death, Eberhart's speaker can hold that some beauty remains at "the guts of things." The speaker in " 'When Golden Flies upon My Carcass Come' " is imagining his body's decay, but he saves the situation from horror by emphasizing the prettiness of the flies that buzz about his "carcass." Their eyes shine upon his body like the sun itself—indeed, they are instruments of the sun—and, though they assemble without conscious thought, they nevertheless function as messengers from time. Since what they convey is a beauty that shines in the very midst of corruption, the poem shows a basis for a spare but assured faith. The adjective clause of the last line—"Which is a fox caught"—could be meant to modify "beauty," in which case it would seem to mean that beauty, which comes from the sun, is sly; or it could be taken to modify "guts," thus implying that man is foxlike. Most probably, however, the clause is meant to modify the whole poem—to suggest that the poet himself is the sly one now captured by death. That he watches the flies suggests, then, that some part of his being survives the death of his body. The fact that the flies work as representatives of sun and time suggests, too, that even physical decay may not be the horrible process men think it.

Eberhart can be even more vigorously outspoken about bodily decay. In "The Virgin," the poet confronts details of physical corruption with an unblinkered eye. It refers to worms, to the putrid, to the mind "disemboweled." Yet it avoids morbidity, partly because Eberhart finds a prettiness—expressed both in content and in sound—even in the most horrifying. Such lines as these are sufficiently graphic but are not ghastly: "The virginal nipples pinched by stones./ The silver belly sullied by slime, ..." The feigned disavowal of intention to dwell on the morbid in line 1 and in lines 13 to 16 is a worn device. But the poem is saved by freshness of imagery, especially in the first twelve lines, and by the vigor of lines 16 to 27 in which the speaker declaims in a neo-Elizabethan rant that is appropriate because sight of the girl is surely sufficient to touch it off. The speaker laments that the girl's physical fate does not differ from that of a beggar; and he then reflects that it is good that he knew her only in "feeling," perhaps meaning that he knew her only in the sense that he felt his kinship with her as a mortal. Memory and perception give her "the lie," try to make him avoid facing the facts of her decay. But, even though they "sue" for his brain, his mind, fevered by sight of corruption, "beats lively as a disease." His mind, that is, works in full awareness of what the sight means. The virgin of the title is not only the girl; it is also the man, now probably for the first time fully aware of the grosser processes of the body's disappearance. The energy of his declamation gives the whole a strength that suggests defiance of death even as he exclaims over its assaults.

Neither "The Young Hunter" nor "Grave Piece" easily yields a meaning. Fortunately, this difficulty is not because of merely private or esoteric symbolism or imagery; fortunately, too, Eberhart has himself written explications of both poems. "The Young Hunter" may be read as a presentation of a mystical identity between the hunter and the bird he shoots (one may recall the theme of Emerson's "Brahma"). The hunter spreads a picnic at which the bird, presumably, is one course, yet an imperative in the third and fourth lines directs the reader to see the bird's blood as representing that in the hunter's own heart. The second stanza declares, somewhat sarcastically, that the central core of nature—represented by a "mary-gold's guts"—is not the equal of the hunter's hard heart and that the core of nature does not magnify its own importance as does the hunter, who now is addressed contemptuously as "hulk that stirs." The sarcasm continues in the third stanza with an allusion to the "nerveless finger" that drew the trigger. The poem changes then, however, to the view that both hunter and dead bird are to be praised, to be seen as aspects of existence. Eberhart's own comment on this poem and this explanation differ in details, but the idea of a transfer of identity between hunter and hunted is the same.[11] It may seem absurd to differ somewhat with the author's own interpretations, but a good poem often supports more than one reading. "The Young Hunter" doubtless will be read in yet other ways.

Eberhart's own explanation of "Grave Piece" is so comprehensive and convincing that one cannot parallel it.[12] In brief, he says that the experience told of is one of "contemplating death," that in this contemplation he became aware of the growth of the "crystal tear" of the "spiritual love which is the

end of contemplation about death." Spiritual love, one deduces, is a love for man and the universe, directed not narrowly to a specific consciousness but comprehensively to embrace both mankind and the mysterious forces that ultimately determine man's destiny.

Eberhart occasionally comments in verse on his practices. "A Meditation" asserts the "cathartic action of beautiful contemplation." Meditating on death, it says, is a "Restorative of the soul," a means for easing the burden that knowledge of mortality imposes on man. The poem is built about the situation of a skull addressing the meditating man who happens to be holding it. In its monologue, the skull comments that action, desire, philosophy are all for the living, that only the dead know the full emptiness of the "terrible void and absolute darkness" to which men come. So too, the skull says, man would not want to know "Of the mind of God, rising like a mighty fire/ Pure and calm beyond all mortal instances/ Magnificent, eternal, everlasting, sweet and mild."

This knowledge of God, one gathers, is too profound, too intimately connected with realizations that would horrify man's limited mind. One may also deduce that the mystery to which Eberhart so often refers lies, perhaps, in the paradox that death is for him a state lacking what man would recognize as either intellect or feeling; yet it is the only one in which realization of divinity can come. The clever situation (reminiscent of Hamlet's meditation on the skull of Yorick, but making the skull the speaker), the melodic statement, and the use of a refrain do not suffice to make the poem important as poetry; but it is of interest for its direct assertion of ideas that Eberhart usually gives obliquely.

Fifteen of the forty-one poems in *Song and Idea* do not reappear in *Collected Poems*. The darkness in human experience is the theme of several of the omitted pieces. " 'Earth Sanctions Old Men' " praises the pity which it finds a characteristic of elderly men. As in *A Bravery of Earth*, we are told that it is in maturity that one learns pity, the "last of human graces" though it is a form of the love that is the "first of human wishes." In " 'My Desire to Write Poetry Without Money,' " the poet tells us that there is no possibility of writing without concern for making a living. He suggests, moreover, that stories of past generations in which poets are said to have lived without economic worry are a trick of the imagination. Though he realizes these economic truths, he finds that "my will, forceful, solemn" continues to

rage; and he asks what a man or poems can do "Against disastrous wars of actuality." Not society or the times, but destiny, the nature of things, is to blame.

Eberhart is critical of contemporary society in the few poems in which he deals directly with it. "Wading Through the Mud of Society" tells how the speaker, laboring through the world, expected to come to "a clean bank" but, instead, sank in imperfection. He grew to love the world, to feel "the elation of a dear psychosis," and became a "moral member of society," one "Giving, for the sake of cash, place, respect/ My hand to life as it is." But his acceptance of society's standards results from "imperfection," for to love this world is madness. " 'Opportunity, Tired Cup of Tin' " is a series of strained metaphors, perhaps owing something to Hart Crane, in which the speaker of the poem finds the Wall Street scene filled with animallike men. Presiding is a blind saxophonist who, like a musical Justice, blows martial notes of retribution while the speaker of the poem moves fishlike in the rigid routine. But even in this poem the social scene is only a surface. Profounder perception shows that through the sordid canyons walks a "triumpher," one "Pouring pity on the world without a murmur." Triumph may be knowledge of mortality; and piety, one sees again, is a quality found in those who comprehend destiny.

In "Anglo-Saxon Song," the speaker tells himself that he must think of man as suffering, must "think" because, apparently, a love affair that ended badly has poisoned his emotions. He must keep his awareness that men's sufferings, the pride and heroism that men resort to, are illusions and vainglorious ornaments. Such activities as conquest, such illusions as peace, must be clung to because he cannot dare to look into "the crooked reach"—the stream of time that would show him the stages by which man's life approaches its doom. Touches of alliteration and some of the diction remind one of Anglo-Saxon verse. The permanence of human destiny is the theme of "For Blake," in which a serpent on a burning lake—a creature and a setting reminiscent of portions of Blake's "Marriage of Heaven and Hell"—prophesies human doom. The last stanza draws an analogy to the "Eternal Snake," presumably time as traditionally symbolized by a snake. As long as time has a future, "There'll be a Burning Lake/ Extending treacheries." One may paraphrase this statement to mean that throughout the human future men will live in a burning lake: their mortality is a permanent condition, not an aspect of a particular era of man's existence.

Three of the omitted poems are too clever. "Realm," dedicated to W. H. Auden, is a series of aphorisms perhaps meant to imitate Blake, but the rhyme is reminiscent of Auden's poem, "This One." Eberhart's lines have neither Blake's freshness of phrasing nor Auden's devices of wit and irony. "Christmas Night" presents a man at a moment of choice, either between two women or between two behaviors; but its suggestion of mystery seems a trick rather than a functional device because the man has already made his decision. A better effort is "The Needle of the Eye," in which three infinitive phrases suggest that "Vigour" and "Growth" are not understood by intellect and that "Reason" cannot attain knowledge of spirit. It would be harder, the poet indicates, for such intellectual efforts to succeed in probing mystery than for the camel to go through the eye of the needle. But the biblical phrasing (Luke 19:25) is reversed in the title, implying that the "eye" is, in this instance, a "needle" which destroys if employed as an instrument of dissection.

Eberhart does not, however, dismiss the possibility of a solely intellectual comprehension only to make the conventional Romantic assumption that emotion or such a quality as love can lead to comprehension. "In "Rumination," he recalls the aging and death of his grandfather and his father; then he muses on the passage of his own life. He concludes that love is not enough to save men or explain their plight, that tragedy comes; and, meanwhile, they cannot be sure whether they "are here to love, or doubt, or pray." The poem is weakened by prosaic lines ("There was an infinite gentleness in his eyes") and by triteness of situation. The inadequacy of neutralism, of a merely blameless life, is shown in " 'Those Who Love Struggle.' " Here the reader is told of men who are heroic because they do not surrender to fate; indeed, they actually love death. They pass through the doubts of early manhood and remain serene through middle age, without the "lustre," the emotional intensity of feeling that a sense of despair would give them. They remain strong even as they contemplate the realization that man dies, calling neither "upon mercy nor upon preachers." But, when death actually nears, their steadiness vanishes as their bodies betray them, and they or their friends ask the tragic question: "where's Love gone?"

The deaths of particular individuals motivate four of the omitted poems. " 'When I Think of Her, the Power of Poetry Arises' " may be compared with the later poem "At Night" in its suggestion that someone long dead can give the poet a benediction in spirit. "Song" recalls the death of an Aunt Nellie Morris who, at the age of eighty, wanted to come downstairs despite a broken hip. Her death, feverish rather than peaceful, intimates that the calm men talk of as an accompaniment of dying is only talk— "the end of a poem." There is a hint of taunting in the closing lines of "Song," for the poet knows that Aunt Nellie's efforts are doomed. The speaker in "Song for the Death of My Uncle in Illlinois" seems to ridicule his own supposed neutralism. While attending the funeral of an uncle he admired but does not mourn deeply, he resolves, somewhat fatuously, to give a word of truth that will impress sightless, thoughtless mankind. But, even as he feels these vain ambitions, the world continues on its course. Parenthetically, the reader is told that he is in truth only an "elf" from the world of commerce—not the grand philosopher he thinks himself to be. These poems about an aunt and an uncle anticipate Eberhart's later verses that characterize individuals.

Death takes the loved, brings down the hearty, fells the admired, and remains beyond the comprehension of the vain-glorious or proud. It arouses in the poet the emotion of " 'In the Night When Destruction Shall Shake the World.' " The speaker sees that a woman he loves is on her deathbed, that the death-rattle is about to "burk" (apparently the equivalent of "burke," a rare word for murder) her. Rather tritely, he remarks that it is "harder to be alive than to be dead." But he recognizes that her eyes have in them a light that intimates something beyond the mundane. He laments the dissolution coming to the "gentle," "small" person who has remained "valid" while the watchers struggled for control and the music of the world broke. The diction (in addition to "burk," the poem uses "fork" and "carking" in somewhat unusual ways) and the strained syntax seem intended to give a note of hysteria.

CHAPTER 3

The Explorer of Dualisms

I *Interinvolvement of Flesh and Spirit*

THE major development in the next decade of Eberhart's work is his willingness to admit, proclaim, and explore a unity of flesh and spirit. Though he showed in such earlier poems as "Suite in Prison" and " 'In a Hard Intellectual Light' " that he sensed this unity, he would not at that time allow himself to declare it. Perhaps his hesitancy arose from influences outside his art. Joel Roache suggests that his marriage and his role as a navy officer in World War II gave him a sense of belonging that helped him leave his introspection of the 1930's and turn toward interests outside himself.[1] Whatever the reasons for the change, one finds him now in "Aesthetics After War" saying that flesh and spirit are "interinvolved"; again, in "Interior Events," he speaks of the relationship as an "interinvolvement." His earlier goal of seizing fire from the heavens to brandish on earth—of proclaiming an inspired superiority to the realm of the flesh—has been replaced by a chastened recognition of man's subjection to destiny and of his own kinship with his fellow men. Eberhart now sees that ideals are not always achieved, that man lives in major uncertainties; and he decides that true knowledge comes only when experienced in the sensory. Though he often alludes to faith in God and Christ, he is independent enough at times to argue that God and man exist in a necessary relationship: man is as necessary to God as God is to man. But, in place of his old determination to seize all of inspiration, to match the bravery of God with the bravery of man, he now thoughtfully admits that man can know only a little of God and of the reasons for man's condition.

Part of his conclusion is that wisdom is a readiness for whatever destiny may bring, a readiness fortified by asurance that death will not mean extinction. Eberhart's man, as presented in "Seals, Terns, Time," is a being pulled toward the future who is as yet held in this world. A creature of his times, he can, however, explore and in part create the times. In his maturity he ceases to disdain this world. He is no longer the frenzied poet seeking to share in the sun, demanding an impossible reincarnation, declaring communion with a pagan earth mother. He is now the subdued but calmly powerful speculative thinker who can conclude that poetry and world should be one and who can say in "Interior Events" that "Universals sit in the flesh,/ Particulars burn in the stars."

But the proof of Eberhart's accomplishment of these years is in the poetry, which includes not only such famous pieces as "The Horse Chestnut Tree" and "The Fury of Aerial Bombardment," but also such fine work as "Seals, Terns, Time," "The Cancer Cells," and "New Hampshire, February." Among many other excellent poems are "Dam Neck, Virginia," "Concord Cats," "'Cover Me Over,'" "Rumination," "Ode to the Chinese Paper Snake," and several sections of "Burr Oaks." This major body of work compels attention to Eberhart's development as an artist.

II *A Unity that Admits Dualisms*: Poems New and Selected

The poetry of this period is brought together in *Poems New and Selected* (1945),[2] *Burr Oaks* (1947), *Selected Poems* (1951), and *Undercliff* (1953). In *Poems New and Selected,* Eberhart prints sixteen poems. Four of these are from *Reading the Spirit* and *Song and Idea.* Of the remaining twelve, nine reappear in *Collected Poems.* Among those retained are two that are deservedly among the best-known American poetry of World War II: "Dam Neck, Virginia" and "The Fury of Aerial Bombardment." Eberhart shows in "Dam Neck, Virginia" his acceptance of the realization that the spiritual may be found in this world. The poem is a meditation on the "beautiful disrelation of the spiritual," on the disparity between the fireworkslike beauty of anti-aircraft fire and the "reality" of the deadly purpose of this show. As projections of man's will, the shells seem to have "a kind of stare," to look back upon the men who watch them. They seem, indeed, to outdo nature because they are cunningly patterned.

But reflection shows that the men whose wills they represent are ignorant of the "vision," the understanding that they arouse in one who watches their effort from some distance away. The watcher's significant realization is not the obvious fact that war in actual experience, in "the animal sinews," is inhuman; it is rather the knowledge that "the spiritual" may be aroused by perception even of cruelty and evil. Attainment of spiritual vision, that is, does not depend upon one's finding daffodils, skylarks, or Grecian urns. It may, indeed, be prompted by experiences that seem unrelated to any action of spirit; and one recalls, in this instance, Eberhart's practice of making poetry from observation of death and decay.

Recognition of the depth of the evil that men may commit drives the poet in "The Fury of Aerial Bombardment" to pose a series of desperate, unanswerable questions.[3] Bombing raids, the speaker says, express such "fury" that one might expect God to relent in what seems to be his hard treatment of his creatures; but there is no relenting and no explanation. One might suppose that, after so many warring centuries, God would cause man to repent; instead, modern man surpasses the original murderer—Cain. What, then, is man to think: was he "made stupid to see his own stupidity"? Is he only the creature of a God who is indifferent to him? Is he in truth an embodiment of "the Beast," an evil that is the real energy of the world?

Having no replies to such questions, Eberhart turns to citation of names of individual men; for one perhaps can hope only to deal with individuals; and, in any case, the waging of war is an activity not of abstractions but of men. In the last stanza, he cites two names which, he says, are only from a list; for they belong to men whose faces he does not recall. The men had themselves died in action soon after learning the nomenclature of their weapons. There is pathos in their deaths, but there is also grim justice in the fact that death may overtake not only those who are targets but often those who do the firing as well. The men represent all of us, and the speaker's sympathy for them as individuals increases rather than lessens the sharpness of his question: what is the nature of the God who permits murder?

The ending is reminiscent of that of "The Groundhog," also a poem in which emotional experience is brought back to the relatively concrete by alluding to particular or named human beings. Now, however, the names chosen are not those of conqueror, sage, and saint but those of ordinary, even indistinguishable, men who are important not for themselves but for the social evil that they represent. The last lines suggest the irony that men who do not know each other's faces can distinguish parts of an ammunition feeding belt. It thereby implies the weight of technical savagery on modern civilization.

A third poem, "World War," is a too-clever contrast of the delights of peace with the horrors of war. The first three stanzas give the glories of "Flutesong willow winding weather"—a fine opening line—when there is no past, only the bright present and future. This hyperwonderful scene is abruptly interrupted by an exclamatory stanza (its second line reads: "Destroy! fracture! cripple! butcher!") which is followed by stanzas giving brutalities of war in words whose first letters are capitalized to suggest newspaper headlines. The point of the poem is so obvious and its verbal cleverness so excessive that its proper uses are propaganda. It was included in *War and the Poet* (1944), an anthology Eberhart edited with Selden Rodman; and it also appeared in an anti-Vietnam war collection.[4]

The verse dialogue "Triptych," later included in Eberhart's *Collected Plays* (1962), is reminiscent of medieval debates between soul and body. Percy, the chief speaker, is a gibing but thoughtful talker whose "food is air", he pokes fun at his own seriousness and exaggerations and pretends to be an Ariel. John, his sober-minded companion, questions him, attempts to restrain his wilder flights, and at times protests; for, no Caliban, he is sympathetic though reasonable. Priscilla, who appears only briefly, feels, with justice, that she is only a foil for Percy's effusions. Partly tongue in cheek, Percy argues for whimsicality and levity while John speaks of reason, tolerance, learning, and lucidity. Percy, however, is shown to be teasing, and John is not made a dull fool: their opposition is not overdrawn. Percy has the best of it poetically, for his lines often have vivid and artful language. Eberhart's best poetry is in a speech that incorporates a version of "The Groundhog" and becomes so strong—to John, so intemperate—that it suggests, as John sees, a belief that death is not the end of existence. Percy defends the artist as one who "saves the world" and, dismissing science, speaks of searching for "the bosom of God." But Percy and John have talked before, and they end now with a recognition that this discussion has not led to conclusions. Percy's position that this world offers nothing significant suggests that the poem is an early one, and Eberhart says in the introduction to *Collected Plays* that it was written in the mid-1930's. "Triptych" is without dramatic action. It is a good display piece for the character of Percy.

Acceptance of this world means abandonment of old idealisms. The speaker in "'Mysticism Has Not the Patience to Wait for God's Revelation'" says that he once sought to attain a point of balance, a mean between extremes, from which he could teach his fellow men courage. But vision, "glimpses in the lightning," gave him saddening knowledge that made it impossible for him to strengthen others. His heart frozen and his moral senses outraged, he concluded that the only certainty is "faith." Visions of classic balance are recognized as enticing in "The Dream," in which the speaker finds himself in a twisting tunnel down which he is drawn by a great light. Suddenly he is whisked into "high regions" of golden harmonies and association with godhead.

But, even as he rather appreciatively recalls these pleasures, he states that they represent "The child's, the death's-head's unconquerable vanity." They are, that is, creations only of the fancy, of man's vain wish for glory. Eberhart can still idealize the dedicated. He admires the "worthy one" of "The Moment of Vision," the man who kept to his "music of the word" despite lack of recognition from the world. The poem describes the gift of vision as a stewardship and—reminding the reader of the title of Eberhart's second volume—declares that "To read the spirit was all my care and is." The speaker loves those who "fight for the spirit," who cling to their esthetic inspirations despite the wrenchings of life. Reliance on "faith" and "inspiration" is consistent with the position that, for illumination, man in his present existence must look to flesh as well as to spirit. As in Eberhart's admission that, though he would like poetry to arrive by inspiration, few poems have actually come to him by that path,[5] he is pragmatic enough to know that man in fact lives most of his time in the world his senses show him.

Acceptance of this world may not mean renewal of optimism; it may, indeed, mean realization of failure. In "Retrospective Forelook" the speaker is a middle-aged man who knows that youthful expectation of a merciful future will be destroyed. The "demon"—knowledge of mortality, one might assume—that takes men out of youthful ignorance drives them not to virtue but to ripened sin. The good days of the speaker's youth were "maskers," deceivers; his pleasures of those times are gone. He remembers his lust for learning and his aspirations to heights he was not to reach. His failure was not only an individual matter: the struggle was one "of all Europe." The eventual victor was Lenin, described as stark yet radiant, "with blood upon his head." Recognizing the importance of Lenin does not make the poem a piece of social verse. Rather, the poet is explaining his inability to arrive at ultimate truths by contrasting the ineffectiveness of all Western thinkers—their metaphysics in a nave—with the success of the hamhanded and bloody but steadfast revolutionary.

But Eberhart, of course, has grounds for optimism. "The Lyric Absolute" presents a man who does not receive the redemption that searches for him. Art, the poet tells the reader, sleeps in a strangeness that is "sounding"—an adjective here used to indicate both that its sleep is noisy and that it is a searching or probing because art seems somehow aware of the warfare in the spirit that surrounds it. Desire, meanwhile, is "sunk in redemption's purifying fire"; but it is not quite yet annihilated. In this world of somnolent art and desire that has been overtaken but not yet conquered, the speaker finds himself "a child/ Who would not be mild,"—a creation of God who willfully resists redemption. In such a world there are two kinds of art, "Images of death" which break up harmony, and "Images of life." Meanwhile, Christ, the embodiment of God, looks for man. The implication is not so much that man actively resists Christ as it is that man is removed from him.

Two poems printed again in *Burr Oaks*, "Song" and "The Preacher Sought to Find out Acceptable Words," are not retained in *Collected Poems*. "Song" suggests that there may be particular missions for men. Four stanzas remark on the influence of each season of the year—paralleling stages of life—upon a meditative man: autumn is when he thinks that he has knowledge; winter is peaceful; spring is inflaming; and summer brings a blooming. But no one of these seasons can bring man to truth. Alternated with these stanzas is a set of four remarking on circumstances of revolutions and wars, events, one deduces, illustrative of men's breaking out of their routine existences. The poem asks then whether the dead are "the same," whether it may not be possible that there is "a special mark in us for a special aim." The intimation seems to be that, since men can have a drive which is not satisfied in any earthly season, and since they have evidence of revolt against things as they have been, it may be possible that "messages" directing men to follow new ways are to be expected.[6]

The values of men who go to war are questioned strongly in "The Preacher Sought to Find out Acceptable Words." Young men at the Pensacola, Florida, Naval Air Station periodically meet "Death the Enemy." The capital letters seem to imply an undue heightening, to hint that men exaggerate the importance of the death of anyone but themselves. When the death of a student pilot comes "out of the blue," unexpected and without understandable reason, the men who witness it are "diverted" only for a moment. Teaching no lesson, pointing no moral, leading to no resolution, the death has no real importance to other men; and even the preacher at the funeral, as the title indicates, gropes to explain. But this seeming lack of significance is itself indicative.

The trainee was at the "summit of . . . goodness," in the youthful period of high dreams. Disregarding this innocence, glorying in his military skill, he became a "descendant from the sky and man," not only one who fell in his plane but also one who allowed himself to forget the "moral imperatives" proper to a man. Failure of other men to recognize these imperatives shows that they share in his guilt. This poem, it may be added, merits preservation.

The one poem in this volume not reprinted in either *Burr Oaks* or *Collected Poems* is "There Is an Evil in the Air," which expresses its speaker's recognition of the ultimate triumph of the terrible" future. This future he believes is sure even though, for the time, he is himself safe on the "ramparts of art triumphal." The poem is unconvincing because it relies on easy rhymes and flat diction.

III *Immortality and Mystery*: Burr Oaks

Burr Oaks (1947) contains thirty poems; ten of these are reprinted from *Poems New and Selected*; and, of the remaining twenty, eleven reappear in *Collected Poems*. Reading these eleven, one is reminded that the content of the "faith" of which Eberhart speaks is principally assurance of continued existence after death. In some poems, he speculates on the form this renewal might take; in others, he is content simply to voice his assurance. One effect of the increased confidence in existence beyond the grave is a sobering. Emotion is now not necessarily lessened, but it is controlled. Both "Rumination" and "'Cover Me Over,'" for example, are moving in their quiet assurance, their lyrical response to the thought of death; but both, traditional in form, work for perfect expression of attitudes shared by other poets rather than for presentation of strikingly individualized emotion.

"Rumination" is a one-sentence poem of eight lines, the first four in iambic pentameter and the last four in iambic tetrameter. This slight shortening of the last four quickens the pace, appropriately so since the lines give a result for the situation described in the first four. The poet says simply that, when he can feel the ultimate chemical rebirth of a rock as soil and flora, he will be "as wise as death" because he will know what death itself knows, that he will be reborn because death will "fire my clay." Death, that is, will take him not to oblivion but to new form— indeed, to form as an object of art.[7] "'Cover Me Over'" also looks to eventual renewal. The speaker, who has died, asks only for concealment and quiet while "night" passes. Short lines, made melodic by careful rhyme and by repetition of key words, give a tone not of protest but of acceptance proper to one who is saddened by realization that death is coming; but he is able to endure because he feels that it will not end all being.

More directly declarative faith in renewed existence is shown in "The Recapitulation" and "'Imagining How It Would Be to Be Dead.'" In "The Recapitulation," not reason but "elation" gives the speaker the feeling that "Death is but a door." He concedes that this feeling may be only a groundless response to desperate hope. But he continues that though, when young, he rejected God, he now, in age, calls on the "Spirit of holy love." Reason must rule in its sphere, but the spiritual also has a sphere. The figure of the door appears again in "'Imagining How It Would Be to Be Dead.'" The speaker tells how he thought of his substance merging with air until he became an almost totally "sentient" being, one given over purely to feeling. Freed from one skull, one earth, he became "the air," a universal spirit. Then, he says, ". . . I pressed on eye and cheek/ The sightless hinges of eternity/ That make the whole world creak." Eternity, it would seem, is like a door that is closed now but is to open someday. This door opens out from the world with a "creak" the "sentient" may hear. Once through the door, one may merge with "eternity."

Earthly fame is not one of the forms renewal may take. "'I Walked over the Grave of Henry James'" is a cool presentation of neutralism—a "balance" of soul that the speaker observed in himself, as, walking by James's grave, he kept one eye on boys at play. He had once disliked James; and, though now conceding that there is value in his work, he easily enough dismisses him to dust and returns to the workday. Not neutralism but love results from the change from early rejection to mature acceptance of "The Ineffable." The speaker says that in earlier years he had not been able to accept the Bible stories of Adam and Eve, or of Cain and Abel, because they seemed merely human inventions. But, as maturity brought understanding, he sensed a spirit of love somewhere in human experience. What matters is "Neither action nor will" but "something glancing off," a mystery of love that lies behind all logic of appearances. One aware of this "ineffable" would not, of course, necessarily accept "old fables"; but he would be receptive to the nonrational.

Questions about human destiny are avoided by the speaker of "'I Will Not Dare to Ask One Question.'" But, though he shuts his mind to the future, experience has taught him that he must die "without answer" to the question that gnaws within him, the question that the reader knows to be, "Why?" The poem is weakened by uncertainties in imagery and rhythm. The question of man's destiny, however, also gives rise to one of Eberhart's major poems, "New Hampshire, February," which speculates that there may be no reason for death to come as it does, that chance has a major role in mortal affairs. The speaker suggests a parallel between the ways of God with man and his own experience with two wasps he found one winter day. He discovered that he could quicken the near-frozen insects by blowing his warm breath on them, or he could let them slip back into torpor by turning away. One enterprising wasp escaped from the pan he was held in and, falling to the floor, was accidentally crushed by the speaker's boot. The other wasp, lacking the energetic intelligence of the first, survived to become a pet.

The moral of this poem is "plain." But the poem will not spell it out, because "You will not like it. And/ God does not live to explain." The "plain" moral is, in part, that intelligence and action do not guarantee achievement of freedom, that one does not earn salvation. Man cannot be sure that his efforts will achieve success, and even God may act by accident. There is humor in the poem's serious treatment of two insects, but it is a grim humor that recognizes man's inability to control destiny. The success of the poem comes partly from its simple but apt analogy, its persuasive matching of circumstance and emotion.

The poems "Ode to the Chinese Paper Snake" and "Burr Oaks" show Eberhart at a stage of mature recognition. Though neither poem has the fire of his best pieces, both show his developed ease with language and with philosophical meditation. "Ode to the Chinese Paper Snake" is an eighty-line poem, a long one for Eberhart. The object of the title, a paper toy on a stick, fascinates the speaker because one holding it can imagine himself to be in godlike control of its destiny; he can pretend, since the object's motions are an extension of his wishes, that he has control of his own destiny. The opening stanzas prepare for the poem's philosophizing by reminding the reader that the snake traditionally symbolizes renewed or endless time. The remark about the creature's interest as a piece of exotica known neither in Maine nor in Vienna is a hint, one assumes, that no deliberate Freudian symbolism is intended. The second section suggests the parallel with man; for, as a mystic would have it, Eberhart finds the object's force strongest when it is nearest to stillness, and he assures the reader that its naturalness, its "parody" of man's own state, is not the product of intellect.

But the poet recognizes that the notion that one can control his destiny is an "effrontery" to knowledge, an "invitation of evil" from what is after all only a toy. With its false intimation that death may be avoided, the device reminds the speaker of his own ties to the human, the mortal; again, he recognizes that to heed the temptation of the snake is to poison himself, though he may be blinded to this by love for himself. The delight of this "destroyer," indeed, is so persuasive that one might perceive its essence as musical, as fabulous sound—an idea conveyed in lines cleverly worded to suggest oddities of sound (especially in lines 3 and 4 of Section VII). This tempter of course gets all its power from man's own imagination, corrupted as it is by desire for immortality. Thus the toy maintains the illusion that one can control his fate, though its energy comes totally from the man who has adroitly projected upon it his own "fantasy." Whatever prophecy the snake may give is only what the man who twirls it reads in it, for it is man who constitutes the eye of the snake and controls its perceptions. And it is man who hardens its "inviolability," who feeds the delusions which maintain the figure of fantasy that it has become. To pin such a freight of meditation to so delicate a bearer risks the ludicrous. But Eberhart succeeds because he reminds the reader that everything meaningful about the snake comes from the man who holds it and because, though the ideas are varied, he uses a style that, being direct but somewhat relaxed, avoids flat assertion and pomposity.

The 171 lines of the title poem "Burr Oaks" present an acceptance of destiny, illustrating this by meditating on scenes associated with the poet's boyhood home (the family property in Austin, Minnesota, was known as "Burr Oaks"). There is no evasion of knowledge, though there are moments of bucolic sentiment. As the reader of Eberhart might anticipate, the series of seven sections opens with celebration of "the intoxicants of things" and ends with meditation in a cemetery. The first section, "The Jungle," finds "secret strength" in the animals and vegetation of a patch of overgrown woodland that in some aspects is analogous to man. It is also renewing to him. Not invigoration but escape is the desire in "The Attic," which finds that the attic's helter-skelter assemblage gives rest from the patterns of the larger world, providing a chaos that is "without pain of reality." A somewhat similar holiday is afforded by the trees of "The

Grove," a wood which seems a place of Wordsworthian calm
without thought of tomorrows, chance, and death. In "The
Orchard" the poet finds himself saddened; for, though he recognizes that blossoms suggest renewal, he is aware that the intimation is only an "as if," that though the mind may attain a
"delicate balance of belief" the particular blossoms that one has
once loved are dead and gone.

"The Barn" contrasts the erratic behavior of man with the
placidity of cows, a placidity that one could come to if he were
to let the mood of acceptance dominate him. Though one should
guard against the danger of becoming bovine, he can continue
to admire the cow's indifference to fate, its concentration on
the immediate. The mood becomes more serious, almost somber,
in "The Pasture." The fields convey some of the enchantment of
the grove and the orchard. But the speaker remembers how,
when a youth, he lay in the pasture to study the mysteries of
the sky; and he realizes that at death too he will lie on the earth.
Nothing, he decides, can be learned if it is "not sensed in earth,"
is not grounded in the recognitions of man's place in the universe
that come when one is in harmony with the fundamental simplicities of earth, grass, and sky.

From this section the poem moves, aptly enough, to the grave-
side musings of "The Cemetery." The twenty-seven lines of
this last section are presented in one sentence, a feat that is
more than a piece of grammarian's cleverness because it suggests
an openness to possibilities rather than a series of "complete
thoughts." One attains "the breathless ease/ Of searching a
high mystery" when conscious of the shortness of life, the
abundance of the world, and the inevitability of death. The
"ease" and the "ecstasy" come when one humbly can be aware
of these constancies yet can say that he accepts, can without
prayer or protest say "let/ Come what may." But acceptance is
not simple. "An Airman Considers His Power" shows the paradox
that the speaker in years of peace was at war—with the self,
or destiny, perhaps—but in time of war finds himself at peace.
In this paradox, he says, "truth has its lease." As in "Dam Neck,
Virginia," the suggestion is that one's moods do not depend on
promptings from outside the self; they may, indeed, differ directly
with what environment or circumstance would seem to instigate.

World War II also gave rise to two poems that are more
prosaic. "At the End of War" is a long prayer, essentially
unimaginative. Though it has occasional original lines (line 6:
"The men in the bureaus mating rubber stamps, carbonizing

history"), it is little more than a versified editorial urging that man's evil be replaced by "love." The poem "A Ceremony by the Sea" is also ultimately prosaic, but its narrative content and pathos of circumstance—it is an account of a Memorial Day ceremony—give it the appeal that comes from ordered report of experience.

The nine poems in *Burr Oaks* that do not reappear in *Collected Poems* include two—"Song" and "The Preacher Sought to Find Out Acceptable Words"—that first appeared in *Poems New and Selected.* Of the seven poems that were first printed in book form in *Burr Oaks* and are not retained in *Collected Poems,* several exhibit the excess of cleverness into which Eberhart, like other poets of great verbal facility, can sometimes fall. "The Peer" reports the speaker dazzled into incandescent bewilderment by the "enormous impinge of things," a perception prompted by watching ants at work. The poem might have survived the grandiosity of its address to the ants as "O little fellows." But it does not have enough impact to make up for the wrenched expression of its last two lines. "The Game" draws an analogy between the poet's search for wisdom and some of the circumstances of a Ping Pong match. The artifice is too obvious. Similarly, " 'My Temples Quake While Fires Exhale' " is a too-clever exploitation of a vague conceit that fires seek the speaker.

"The Magical" and "The Full Weakness of Man" are meditations concluding that "mystery" is the only possibility of salvation. "The Magical" tells, somewhat too cleverly, of a dream in which the poet thinks he is with angels in an existence that cannot be explained methodically. Though pained by the sin and corruption of the body, he decides that the body is necessary because it is all man has to exist in. He says optimistically that "mystery" will lead man away from the errors of his flesh until he comes to see the "evanescence of the morning," the brevity of mortal existence, and to hear the suggestion of such reassurance as that which is said to come from caves revered in Hinduism. In "The Full Weakness of Man," the first seven stanzas report the difficulties of the poet who wishes to be heard by other men. He must talk; but, when he overcomes his early doubts about his own abilities, he finds no one to listen. One can only pity both those who do not hear and the speaker who is filled with "blood so firmly shouting." The resolution is that mystery may come to propose a harmony like that of a wind bearing angels, like that known when "the full weakness of man is a strength." This harmony, one deduces, is comparable to that the poet believes a meditative man may attain when, admitting the inability of his body and intellect to answer the questions of existence, he relies on spirit.

"The Magical" is too clever, but "The Full Weakness of Man" is somewhat prosaic. The poem "Of Truth" is a good performance because its quick pace and its varied figures and modes of expression suggest the anxiety of the speaker's search for truth, a quality that he concludes must be "a vast middle" because it does not seem to lie at any of the extremes he probes. Though in several poems in this volume Eberhart has dismissed the idea of a classical balance as the goal of his search, he nevertheless is moving toward a centralist position. What he wants becomes apparent in later poems in which he finds himself at an active center, held in an alert contention between forces rather than merely balanced. In "Of Truth" there is the light of humor that often in Eberhart's work conveys the idea that his search, though anxious, is not desperate; that the speaker is experienced enough to realize that he is not going to find overt answers.

Perhaps the best of the omitted poems is "Speech of a Protagonist." A figure labeled "The Poet" delivers a monologue in which he reflects that he feels entangled and that English professors pain him. He questions the Latin and Greek, the rigors of school; and he questions "that asylum of affront"—perhaps a school where the poet himself taught—where he fought regimentation but "won some spiritual visitation." This "visitation," he realizes, drives him on. The feeling is ardent enough to bring conviction. Acquaintance with some of the details of Eberhart's career suggests also that the poem is at least partly autobiographical. With its first and fifth lines changed to allude to music, the poem reappears as part of a speech in the play "The Mad Musician."

IV *At Mid-Career*: Selected Poems (*1951*)

All but three of the fifty-three poems in *Selected Poems* (not to be confused with *Selected Poems 1930-1965*) had appeared in one or another of the earlier books. Of these three, only "Brotherhood of Men" reappears in *Collected Poems*. In this monologue a veteran of the American surrender at Corregidor in 1942 realizes, after reflecting upon his sufferings, that during difficult times men deal more directly with each other—even though necessary cunning includes overlooking mistreatment of a friend—and are closer to truth than they are in times of peace. Though less intense, the paradox is similar to that explored in "An Airman Considers His Power." In form, the monologue borrows from Old English verse, using marked alliteration and in most lines a strong caesura. It lacks drama, however; it is overlong for the point it seeks to make; and it is weakened by "poetic" moralizing in its next-to-last stanza. But its details, undoubtedly drawn from accounts of survivors, are exact and graphic.

Both of the pieces omitted from *Collected Poems* ponder the problems of achieving unity. "Dissertation by Wax Light" shows the difficulty of achieving harmony between two lovers. The speaker recognizes that each party in the affair was using the other to satisfy himself, even though each thought that in rapture they had become one. But time, and the afflictions of pride and jealousy, destroyed the seeming unity. Until men can divorce love from desire, the reader is told, the only lasting unity is in God. One may note Eberhart's continued suspicion that desire, the will, blocks attainment of harmony and purity.

After a pleasant day on a Wisconsin lake, the speaker in "At Lake Geneva" comes across a travel article by D. H. Lawrence that first reminds him of his own travels in Sicily, then sets him to musing on whether anyone still pays attention to what Lawrence wrote. (The time is apparently the mid-1930's. The travel article is said to date from 1929 and to be seven years old. Lawrence died in 1930.) The speculation arouses in the speaker a "loathing" for time. He is somewhat taken aback by the fact that he is jarred out of his reverie by so slight a thing as a passing sound, but he returns to musing on the coincidence that both he and Lawrence had been in Sicily. Though the speaker seems to feel that there is significance in this "conjunction," he cannot find it and is left wondering about the relevance of the imagined.

In another Wisconsin summer, this time at Washington Island, he reflects that "What immediately surrounds us is real," that the phenomena of the visible world are good. Activities at the moment are elemental, without subtleties; they are represented by the worn joking of a pair of "clown" friends, hourly beer, and the sight of the Northern Lights. The speaker decides that he needs to be either bigger, perhaps godlike, or littler, less imaginative: the human being is caught between grandeur and smallness. He will settle for small happiness, letting the "problem of Form" go for a while because it is ridiculous to expect the "Esemplastic," the power to unify seeming disparities by use of the imagination. The skill with which the poem employs physical circumstance without becoming prosaic and the importance of the questions it raises would justify including it in future collections.

V *Continued Probings*: Undercliff

The volume *Undercliff* (1953), named for the Eberhart summer home in Maine, illustrates the range of Eberhart's meditations. More important, it shows him in command of his art, able to make compellingly moving poetry about such favorite themes as reassurance, the plight of man, the importance of chance, and the intensity of spiritual ardor. Of the volume's fifty-nine poems, twenty-four appear in *Collected Poems*. The Romanticism of Eberhart's early work is illustrated by "Indian Pipe," a poem that in concept and form is reminiscent of Freneau's "The Indian Burying Ground." That it should be conventional, rather too "poetic" is understandable when one learns that Eberhart wrote it when he was sixteen or seventeen.

How one characteristic of Eberhart's early work is carried on in his maturity is illustrated in " 'Go to the Shine that's on a Tree,' " a lyrically passionate cry for inspiration. The poet urges his hearer, or himself, to go to the glory he sees in a tree washed in the light of dawn; to listen to the song of a bird that shares that wonder; finally to "Be tree and bird," to merge for an ecstatic moment with the natural world in order to take part in the glory the sky has given it. One notes that man is to merge with nature, not to escape from it. Such moments of glory are rare.

" 'Sometimes the Longing for Death' " states that it is hard even to wish for "Imaginative death," a state which is reached not in the physical process of dying but in moments when one senses "supernatural love." In such death, one feels a "New life" which is not afflicted with pain-bringing hope. The poem asks whether it is for "this"—for nothing more than this, is the implication—that life takes man through its wrenching cycles.

"At Night" reassures the reader that in moments of vision one can attain imaginative touch with the extranatural. Standing on the beach, at the edge of the sea of life, the speaker finds that he does not understand the death of his parents, which presumably took place some years before. Yet love comes to him, a love that seems to intimate their presence though he knows intellectually that their bodies are dust. Thought of disease and death is at "rest," and somehow he feels "from the sea" his parents' "presences": they seem alive in spirit and almost in flesh

84 RICHARD EBERHARTRICHARD EBERHART

as well. The rhythm makes for an incantatory effect of wonderment, one that gives Eberhart an assurance more profound than logic could provide. This contact with wonder again comes through the physical, here through the sea; and the very sense of his parents' appearance is "terrene."

But neither ecstasy, questioning, nor reassurance can allow the poet to blink at what he sees as the facts of human destiny. "A Love Poem" suggests, somewhat in the manner of Emerson's "Brahma," that its speaker is the moods and qualities he senses —lightness, terror, question, dream. This speaker tells the reader, indeed, that unless he could find "comfort" in his environment he would find his mind taken away. Such speculations, he adds, raise philosophical questions about the substantiality of the world and the flesh. But all this is broken off by the skepticism, almost the despair, of the last stanza as the poet recalls that "Love" gave him an answer. Though he does not say directly what this answer was, one gathers from the allusion to worms and from the statement that the question was "evaded" that Love has reminded the speaker that answers, if any, can only be attained by going through the process of death. Once more, the path to the spiritual takes one through the physical.

The next four poems in the *Collected Poems* give an interesting range of approaches. "God and Man" is a prosaic, awkward piece of reasoning; "The Horse Chestnut Tree," a deservedly famous expression of wonder and recognition; "The Tobacconist of Eighth Street," a moving presentation of the effect of another man's death; and "Seals, Terns, Time," an apt use of natural objects as symbols in a meditation on man's condition. "God and Man" shows the poet in youth—his family relationships and his opportunities. As he matures, it appears that angels may guide him; but time brings evil. In the first and third stanzas, the speaker's arrival at physical adulthood is indicated by the remark that he is "a man." By the sixth stanza, he is "Man"— the capital letter indicating, one gathers, that with the chastening knowledge that comes with maturity the speaker has come to represent all of mankind. By this stage, one has lost not only relatives and youthful dreams but also even the sense of loss. One ripe for destiny comes to know the insubstantiality that makes even death "only another dream." God, the reader is told, controls everything. It follows that "To be God God needs man/ As man needs God to be man." The poem is notable for its forthright talk of God, but it is too crammed with semitheological speculation.

"The Horse Chestnut Tree" has the esthetic virtues lacking in "God and Man." Its details and its tone contribute to the effect of wonderment, an acceptance of paradox which rises to celebration instead of becoming mired in rationalization. The poem expresses the poet's wonder at the "great flowering world" created by "the lawgiver," as well as something of the sadness of his realization that man can acquire only "a little handful" of knowledge about this world. The boys who try to rob the tree are "lawless," yet follow a law all the same—the law that impels men to seek that which is most beyond them. Trying to reach the topmost nuts, instead of waiting for time to bring them down, the boys are not satisfied with the portions of God's world that are accessible to them. The speaker, an adult, must order the boys to leave though he remembers that in his own youth he too robbed chestnut trees. In maturity he sees the analogy between looting boys and philosophizing men: both seek a "good" from "the unknown." Evening drives off the boys, as death will end the questing of men, "outlaws on God's property." There is no explanation of the universe's impenetrability and man's desire. The poem gives an earned harmony, an acceptance which, far from resignation, is a presentation of beauty that is experienced rather than intellectualized.

Reason and acceptance do not always prevail, of course. In "The Tobacconist of Eighth Street," emotion overpowers the speaker. Finding that a tobacco dealer he had traded with had suffered a "collapse of affairs," of body as well as of business, the poet "went howling"; he was "Smashed with recognition," and he "sent a useless prayer." Honesty, not hypocrisy, tells him that "Such insight is one's own death rattling past." He had never had any closer relation to the tobacconist than that of customer. Yet he cries out for him, partly because he is a fellow man, but principally because he knows that the "collapse" anticipates his own.

Man's situation as a being caught between flesh and spirit is movingly presented in "Seals, Terns, Time," a poem that draws on suggestions of the half-mythical past, on objects of nature, and on aspirations for the future. While rowing near Western Isle—near Eberhart's summer home in Maine—the speaker sees seals at play in the tide, which is identical with the "burden of our strange estate." He sees not only the animals themselves but also their "images," significances beyond their physical being. These seem the "deep elapses of the soul," an "ancient blood" akin to that of man's own sea-born ancestry. As the poet med-

itates on prehistory, his eye is drawn to the terns whose "aspirations dip in mine." The result is a moment of both static balance
and active contention in which he feels that "I am in compulsion
hid and thwarted,/ Pulled back in the mammal water,/ Enticed
to the release of the sky." He is held by his human associations,
by all the past history of man as a mortal creature of the flesh;
yet he is equally compelled toward the future, "enticed" by the
world of spirit. The poem carries conviction because it presents
an understanding of man's situation that is esthetic rather than
merely philosophical or editorial. The poem's rhythm has not
only enough of the incantatory to impart the strength of its
meditation, but also enough energy to show that the poet is
indeed pulled two ways rather than held in a merely passive
balance.

The artistic appeal even of one of the instruments of man's
death, and the arbitrary and overpowering destiny that brings
that death, are subject matter for "The Cancer Cells," "Forms
of the Human," and "Oedipus." In "The Cancer Cells" Eberhart
develops an analogy between the cells and the artist's mind and
the "murderous design" of the universe itself. Menacing to the
imaginative, mere phenomena to the neutral observer, the cells
suggest resemblances that appeal to the artist. Leonardo da
Vinci, the reader is told, " . . . would have in his disinterest/
Enjoyed them precisely with a sharp pencil." As with Eberhart's
exploitation even of decaying bodies, he shows here remarkable
ability to make fine poetry from subjects usually regarded as
morbid and repulsive. His suggestion of resemblances convinces
by its truth, and his control of detail and style produces a unified
work of art. Rather than attempting to rise above the flesh, he
makes art by concentrating on it.

"Forms of the Human" and "Oedipus" work at a much lower
level of intensity. The poet says in "Forms of the Human" that
he once felt that he did too much thinking and that he meant
to correct himself by means of his knowledge. But what he
actually did was an act not of intellectualism but of emotional
symbolism: he planted three beans and preserved the one that
came up "wild." The poem suggests that the poet values the
free and emotional rather than the intellectual and conventional.
It also suggests, somewhat like "New Hampshire, February," that
chance may determine survival. "Oedipus" first criticizes the
king named in the title by remarking that he could not improve
"insight" by his act of blinding himself; then it reflects that one
cannot "unravel" fate but only "accept" it. Additional meditation

leads to the conclusion that Oedipus, like all men, was caught in "the universal drench," the all-powerful tide of destiny.

"Fragment of New York, 1929," is unusually long for a poem by Eberhart, extending from page 113 to page 122 in the *Collected Poems*. At four-thirty on a morning late in October, the speaker goes along the street to his work in "the factory," which is in truth a slaughterhouse (probably similar to the one Eberhart worked in briefly in 1929). Pages 115 to 118 give a graphic picture of the killing and processing of animals for meat, frequently making use of sexual imagery to suggest violation of dignity, and drawing a direct comparison between the inability of the animals to avoid their fate and the inability of man to escape his doom. The poet moves to the roof of the building and then apparently to a café, but his thoughts return to the slaughterhouse as he reflects on comparisons between the beauty of the city's harbor and the inner organs of animals, on the unthinking strength and the human vulnerability of those who deal out death, and on his own role as an observer.

The conclusion is not a continuation but a meditative passage: sudden change—the stock-market crash of 1929, one deduces—has ended the enterprise. The poet sees the slaughterhouse scene as typifying the era that produced it—a time of "savage complexity," of "The harsh omnipotence of evil." Although the poem is presented as a monologue, its shifts in approach make for weakness in unity. But several passages are well done. The lines on page 114, for example, in which the poet goes through the city streets are given in an appropriately nervous, abrupt syntax that suggests the wrought up state of his emotions. The poem is also of interest as one of the few in which Eberhart expresses a fairly direct view of the state of society.

Though not important as a poem, "Aesthetics After War" is a good illustration of the way Eberhart attempts to work out answers to important questions. The poem, covering just over six pages, is a meditation on questions similar to those that often engaged Wallace Stevens; but its content is in line with Eberhart's own ideas rather than an imitation of Stevens. The first of the four sections, "Propositions," questions the ways observers of differing casts of mind may view the world, asking whether any of them come to truth. It ponders the relation between thinking and contemplation, between truth and beauty, and be-tween esthetics and morality—this last a question raised especially in connection with the beauty sometimes said to be perceived in events of war. The second section, "Instruments," recognizes the marvel of such achievements as the Mark 18 gunsight and the radar screen, devices that belong to "a bewildering array of imaginations." But the poem reminds the reader that these marvels are not essentially mysterious but are inventions by men.

The question of importance is whether these objects of human devising are in any way superior to man himself, whether they contain an extra element beyond that he has given them or whether some perhaps unrecognized capacity in himself gives them their marvelousness. This question leads to another: is there mystery in the world outside man, or does all mystery arise from what "the Deity" has put in man himself? The third section, "The Pull of Memory," suggests that mystery is at the heart of truth by remarking on the necessity of opposites, citing as one authority Jakob Boehme, the German religious mystic. The section illustrates this necessity by implying a comparison between Chinese in an opium haze—representing oriental mankind—and the "selfless" spirit of Buddha; and it concludes that orientals get rid of the self when contemplating whereas men of Western society cannot even in contemplation escape intrusions of the self. The implication is that neither easterner nor westerner has the whole truth, that truth may lie with both, or in some tension or area between the two.

The fourth and longest section, "Reality," specifies, however, certain definite realities: death, in the case of aerial gunners; love, for Saint Teresa; "identification," for Boehme; innocence and experience, for Blake. At least in the case of aerial combat, chance plays a large role in human destiny. Awareness of this reality raises the moral reflection that the death of one man, even though an enemy, diminishes the mankind that "Christ shed his blood for," the mankind of which each of man is a part. Christ knew the evil in each man and would redeem both gunners. Because all things are interrelated—estheticism with philosophy, philosophy with life and action—so Christ was "the most aesthetic man." The poem decides that the poet achieves the timeless, is mystically a part of what he contemplates, the giver of "insight" and practitioner of an art in which man's spirit rises.

The questions of the opening section about the effect variations in the mind of the perceiver may have on his understanding of what he perceives have been answered not by direct rationalism but by progress to recognition that all aspects of creation are "interinvolved," with Christ at the center. Man's own nearest approach to Christlike perfection is through poetry. The second section, and to some degree the first, are rather too prosaic; but the poem avoids the tortured syntax of some of Eberhart's ventures at reasoning in verse. A passage at the opening of the second section makes poetry out of a seemingly forbidding subject: description of a gunsight.

Another study of esthetic questions, a poem rather more reminiscent of Stevens in setting and style, is "The Verbalist of Summer." The "verbalist" at the shore considers how to "wash," to comprehend the significance of the sea. He asks whether "the real sea" is that of colors and transparencies that his eyes show him, the "chasm" of story and myth, or a "Messenger" from nature to man. When the trance induced by his study clears, he recognizes that he is "natural," that his intellect is artifical, a "super-imposition." In the eight stanzas of the poem's second section, the verbalist first tells himself that he is master of the sea, that it is what he imagines it to be; he tells himself, indeed, "I am the sea." Yet all the while he is somehow mindful that he is "actually, foreign to this element" and that the sea is a reality beyond his art. Having failed to reconcile these diverging understandings, the verbalist in the seven stanzas of the final section makes one last attempt to control the sea but comes to recognize its power—its constant escape from his attempted impositions of "order." He concludes that to be "didactic" about the sea is to be only a child—and a child sees of the sea only "the bright pebbles by the shore." The suggestion may be that the child sees only a narrowly limited view; or it may be that the child's view in its acceptance and concreteness is the best that man may achieve. One may note that Stevens' poem "The Idea of Order at Key West" also suggests possibilities rather than coming to firm conclusions.

Although the esthetic questions are serious, the Latinate diction throughout suggests that Eberhart is lightly mocking the "verbalist" for attempting a "didactic" understanding. Eberhart succeeds, but at a lesser level than Stevens, for this poem lacks the color and especially the air of authority Stevens could give verse about such topics. Eberhart's professional skill enables him to write reasonably well in this mode, but speculation on esthetics is not his forte.

More zestful writing gives impact to "On Shooting Particles Beyond the World," a poem inspired by early efforts of the United States to fire objects into orbit in space. The poem mocks man's "empirical delusions," his efforts to imitate the powers of God by "imbecile" efforts to move beyond his proper realm. If man would open his eyes to the "the comforts" of his existence, the spiritual inspirations that await him here, he would attain wisdom. But man continues to shoot metal into the sky and to wish that he himself might escape the earth. The atom bomb "accepted this world," was limited in its effects to the earth; now man seeks to "spit" on the sun itself. But it is not God that man will find in space: man's enterprise only confirms his imperfection; his cry of triumph is a hiss like that of the snake in Eden. The poem uses puns, satire, and apt diction and analogies to sustain its strong, effective ridicule of man's pretensions.

A contrast in tone and purpose is "A Legend of Viable Women," a four-page poem slightly reminiscent of François Villon's "Ballad of the Dead Ladies." Eberhart's purpose is largely playful. His speaker describes a variety of women, and one implication seems to be that, though man may roam in his imagination, he is always tied to the flesh. The citation of women of the past also suggests Eberhart's frequent theme of the mortality of man, but the use of women characters provides a novel angle of attack on the theme. The last two sections turn more serious. Women, the reader is told, are crushed by time as all mankind is; they are "the flesh" sharing with man the experience of reality, yet they also represent the mother to whom he must always ultimately return, the earth of which he is made. The poet now hails a maternal principle exemplified by human women; he no longer seeks a pagan earth mother.

A related theme is the integrity of nature, an idea suggested in "Concord Cats." The animals of the poem are in harmony with nature, aware that it is "meant for poise." The wars and death of men, one is told, are only transistory events. Reality and truth are represented by aspects of the natural world: "The stars blue, the night paling—/ Are data. Imperviousness. Integrity." The implication, of course, is that men fail to perceive the simple, concrete realities an animal knows by instinct.

"On the Fragility of Mind" is a slighter piece, beginning with the seeming praise that the mind is "delicate evidence," but then calling it "dense" and "foxy," and finally suggesting that perhaps "there is no mind at all" but only emotions and art. The poem is, of course, a speculation on one extreme position of antirationalism. It makes a suggestive contrast with Marianne Moore's "The Mind Is an Enchanting Thing," a poem that in its salute to the mind's charms admits its importance as well as indicates its limits.

"Great Praises"—the title poem of a later volume—is an attempt at the expression of the same ardor that fills " 'Go to the Shine That's on a Tree.' " But in "Great Praises" the opening ecstasy turns toward the somber as the speaker says that he has learned to love the "order," the compelling flush of summer that in "intellectual pride" he formerly rejected; but the shift in approach is awkward. "The Dry Rot" also is weakened by a shift in point of view. Discovering decay in the heart of some wood, the speaker refers to it sarcastically as the "rare old stuff of mankind's dream." The too-prosaic second stanza suggests philosophical speculations that might arise and remarks that time is the dry rot found in blood. Instead of going ahead with speculation, however, the speaker relates that he smeared the substance on himself; like Anthony, he went to Egypt where he met "a savage queen"; and, giving up on efforts at comprehension, he turned to the flesh. He closes with a half pathetic, half defiantly sarcastic appeal to the future: when men unearth his bones, they should think "of dialetic, imagination, the Rose of Venus"—should ponder the relationships between mind and love. The poem's ultimate effect is a fatalism that suggests that neither thought nor love can give man control over destiny.

Fatalism is not a usual mood in Eberhart's work, however. More typical are the exuberance and humor that in "The Skier and the Mountain" cause him to recognize his limitations. The speaker feels that he is like a skier who can imagine himself attaining the summit where "the gods" reside, but he knows that imagination is too frail a wing to raise him. Thus he is the victim of the imagination, one led on by it but without ability to direct it. He tells of a "vision" in which he saw "an old country god of the mountain" who vanished as he was about to ask an intellectual question, perhaps about a meaning for human existence. The gods lead men toward themselves, suggest infinite possibilities, but finally "keep their secrets." At least while man remains man, he cannot achieve understanding of them. The poem uses a colloquial style that gives it a touch of mild humor which serves to prevent the mood from slipping into melancholy or despair. The poet sees that there would be no point to tears and desperation.

"The Human Being Is a Lonely Creature" declares a problem for which "The Book of Nature" offers a solution. Pain is "essential," and all men fear it because "Death is waiting for the human creature." Love and harmony can help men endure, but death nevertheless will come. In style and effect the poem is close to a prose editorial. Use of a near refrain does not sufficiently elevate it above the merely didactic.

"The Book of Nature"—in the volume *Undercliff,* though not in *Collected Poems,* the title is followed by the inscription "Undercliff 1952"—tries more successfully to elevate by repetition of the words "As," "And," and "An" as line openings; the effect is appropriately similar to that of a litany. The solution the poem offers to man's problem is God. While the speaker makes his daily round at the New England coast, he comes in a visionary moment to sense himself as "Holding all things together," to feel that he sees God "on my fingertip." Anticipations of death are forgotten, and he feels "glad for all who ever lived," no matter what his mind may tell him. God provides him with "an answer." That he receives one is indicated both by the speaker's sense of joy in his experience and by his allusion to a process of "wrath and judgment." To this speaker, at least, the existence of God promises joy after a time of trial.

Undercliff's first section contains fourteen poems which are not reprinted in *Collected Poems.* The best of these is "Sea Scape with Parable," written in the odd style that Eberhart's authority and energy keep from seeming quirky. The poem inevitably reminds one of Robinson Jeffers's "The Purse-Seine" in its explicit analogy between fishermen who are hauling in their nets, and "the Fisher King, who with the net of time" draws men themselves to death. Just as fish sometimes escape, so does man; but, the last stanza warns, death will win. "What if Remembrance?" is interesting for its similarity to poems by H. D., both because it asks a prettily pathetic question and because it comes to an end in two one-word lines. "Chant of the Forked Lightning" and "One Way Dialogue" comment on man's imprisonment in the flesh, the first regretting in playful style that man will never achieve the sure validity of natural objects and experience, the second insisting on recognition that one can never escape the self and his own flesh. The poem "Reality! Reality! What Is It?" exclaims, rather too flatly, over the speaker's doubts and desperations and his attachment to Christ. The source of his desperation is the mortality whose inevitability is meditated upon in "Wisdom," one of the best of the omitted poems. "The Poet-Weathervane" remarks on the "damage of the centuries," the replacement of natural response to inspiration by modern use of intellect.

"The Look" somewhat anticipates the poem "May Evening" in meditating on what the world will be like following a man's death and in speaking of what his survivors will feel. In "Baude-laire," the poet recites the French poet's struggles to achieve expression, but the poem says in its ending that he failed because he did not honor "Love, the source." In contrast, the speaker of "Indian Summer" finds himself "blessed" with richness in the autumn of his life, accepting and loving his environment and his role in it. That poems as competent as "The Look" and "Indian Summer" could be omitted from *Collected Poems* is evidence that Eberhart's standard of accomplishment has become very high indeed.

In "That Final Meeting," yet another reflection on deathbed reality, the speaker finds that the scene suggests mystery without sentiment, a "brute recognition" only. In "Order and Disorder," another assertion that the answer to the problem of mortality is Christ, the Christ is the wild passion, the one great figure who escapes the bounds of total—and therefore limited—harmony. "Soul's Reach" expresses a conventional religious position: the speaker cannot "cry Yea" until he has learned to "say Nay": only by learning to rid himself of desire, almost of hope, can he be fully receptive to God. His situation is that of the speaker in "Chiliasm" (the title refers to the doctrine that before Judgment Day Christ will reign on earth for a thousand years). Such a reign is for the future, the poem implies. The speaker, meanwhile, is caught between God and the Devil; he is both "Love" and "Wrath."

Four of the poems in *Undercliff's* second section are not reprinted. "War and Poetry" is perhaps Eberhart's most thoughtful comment on the relationship of war to poetry. Though Eberhart himself wrote some of the best poems in English to come out of World War II, he says that the war was "rot of imagery," that poetry should arise not from "extravagance" of war but from "the things we lost" in wartime—the shells and leaves and testaments of harmonious moments. Poetry, he concludes, should be "calm, massive"; it should consider "The welfare of the inner ecstasy,/ Inviolable voice of universal form." Solemn and thoughtful, the poem actually seems too much a deliberate attempt to express what one may suspect Eberhart thinks one ought to feel. The fact that he had already come to believe that poetry is in part a product of "the flesh," and his own success with such work as "The Fury of Aerial Bombardment," suggest that the esthetic position of "War and Poetry" is not an accurate presentation of his views.

Among longer poems are "Choosing a Monument," "Letter I,"

and "A Man of Sense." "Choosing a Monument" is a discussion
among the brothers Rogers and Philip and their sister May
in which love is shown as more important than intellectual
position. Roger and May wish to sell a parcel of land in the
dry Southwest; but Philip, a man who is concerned with time
and vision and who wishes to keep the land, vaguely supposes
it may be a refuge against society or, perhaps, prove to have
some new unseen commercial worth. When Roger proposes
that they use the proceeds from the sale to build a marble
monument over their parents' graves, Philip objects that to
do so would glorify death, that love lies in the heart, and that
the land itself would be a better bond with the parents. But
he surrenders, concluding that by agreeing with the others
he is helping forge a bond of love among the three of them
and that the vain monument is at worst only irrelevant.

"Letter I" salutes the artist as the man who by imagination
brings temporary order to man's chaotic experience. Philosophers, and intellectuals generally, have been put to shame
by natural man—by the aircraft mechanic who is the modern
counterpart of Wordsworth's leech gatherer and, of course,
by Christ. The poles of experience are represented by the
musician, in whose art men do not have to think but only "be,"
and the scientist, described as a measurer who is not content
until he builds an all-consuming bomb. The harsh words are
apologized for in the recognition that science and poetry "come
from the trunk . . . the seed of man." The speaker praises the
philosophical anarchist, saying that he is a preserver of freedom.
He explains that the mind is to be respected but that it is not
the highest of capacities because it leads men to despair in the
face of death. If life were "euphoria," he continues, men would
not be doomed; but the fact is that none escape death. He
praises poetic creation as an act of mystery and, apparently as
an analogy, describes the Pacific sea lion and other ocean
creatures as exemplifying patience and grace; and he finds
in desert scenes a natural music and painting.

These reflections lead to the question, "What is art?" There
is, the speaker says, an indistinguishable line between will and
destiny; but men cannot know to what extent they choose, to
what extent they are impelled to act. But men may define the
terms: will is "the driving ego"; destiny is "the fate of the times
surrounding you." These two energies are in dramatic conflict
of which art is "a momentary resolution." The speaker extends
his description, saying that the will, inherited from ancestors,

is the consequence of individualism. Since the artist cannot escape his times and his art, the result is a "relative capability" (a term surely intended to suggest comparison with Keats's "negative capability"). Eberhart adds speculation on the extent to which Dante and Shakespeare were in the grip of their times, deciding that the artist reflects both his age and his own "state of grace," his own inspiration. The final passage describes the twentieth-century artist as one who seems a toy of fate, a likely victim of war, family tragedy, or economic catastrophe. He may choose among various positions—nihilist, Communist, experimentalist, religious believer, and others—but, in any case, is caught in his times. But he is no worse off than the artist of other times. And those artists struck by "greatness" are, now as ever, dominant over their age, "Creating its very nature in its retrospect,/ Its flavour, its temper, its oddity, its peculiarity." If the poem is too prosy for most tastes, it is thoughtful, clear without being simplified, and gives an excellent representation of Eberhart's intellectual and esthetic positions in the early 1950's.

"A Man of Sense," an appealing picture of the imaginative man, is presented with affection and underlying humor. One recognizes Eberhart himself in the portrait, and may pair the poem with "Letter I" as a stock-taking. The man of sense sees "God and evil" but does not "go mad over inscrutability" and is sufficiently detached from events and tradition to follow his own imagination. He has outgrown the Romantic, becoming a Classicist, if by that one means that he values balance and harmony. He has three possible stances: he may resemble the Athenian in being purified by experience of tragedy; he may be like the idealistic Christian, prizing an inner unity; or he may simply be realist enough to inhabit "the actual world," in which case he will have "made it in his senses by imagination free." The absence of "A Man of Sense" from *Collected Poems* should not lead to its disappearance.

Seventeen of the twenty-four poems in Part III of *Undercliff* are not reprinted in *Collected Poems*. One of the best is "An Herb Basket,"[9] a poem which first appeared as a pamphlet and, like "A Man of Sense," should be retained in collections. The speaker muses on the goals of poetry in a series of twenty stanzas that vary in mood from the playful and inquiring to the serious and the melancholy. He decides that the passage of time brings regret not only because it entails losses but also because it dulls response to events. He will walk in dark woods because in that atmosphere he can renew some of the feeling time has dulled—a conclusion that suggests one reason for Eberhart's frequent emphasis on the seemingly morbid. A related theme informs the eighteen stanzas of "Phoenixes Again," in which, after musing upon the way two poets once read Shakespeare, the speaker declares that his goal will be to praise the spirit and subdue the mind; and, by this arrangement, he will find it possible to praise "Order, calm, and luxury."

The professional competence Eberhart had developed by this period could at times become a mere technique, a manner that could be applied endlessly. "Lines to an Old Man" is typical of his work in its concern with the approach of death and its allusions to cosmic realities; it is also typical in being lyrical meditation, neither stern nor comforting. But it lacks the freshness of insight to make it distinctive. "To My Son, Aged Four" and "Order Again" are equally competent—and equally routine. "Elusive Concretions" is less polished, but it is a better poem because it makes its point about the passage of time by means of a series of specific examples.

The poem as a written artifact is the topic of four poems. "Furtive Marks on Paper" praises the poet by suggesting that his penstrokes may speak "for the dignity of man." "To One, Who, Dead, Sees His Poems in Print One Hundred Years Later" shows the dead poet still unsatisfied—not at failure on his own part but at the continuing lack of adequate comprehension of the chaotic world. "Calligraphy" draws an analogy: is the poem when off the page perhaps comparable to the soul when out of the body? Can the one be without the other? What one might hope a poem could accomplish is shown in "The Lost Poem" as a writer searches desperately for the verse that had "vision and control," that "Bestrode imagination" and "mated" good and evil. One may hope, again, that in future compilations Eberhart, or his editors, can find room for work with the thoughtful energy of "The Lost Poem."

Eberhart makes interesting use of concrete perceptions in "Motion as Grace," which praises a woman's subtle movements, and in "Grape Vine Shoots," which honors the certainty represented by the vine. In "Pleasures of the Morning," perception of a blue jay taking off from a daffodil brings the poet back from cloudy imaginings of "the general" to an awareness that is informed by tangible reality. That neither men nor their physical environments change is the message of "The Great Stone Face"; only poetry invents "the new possibilities." A similar idea comes by comparing "The Dream of Time," which pictures man as captive of time as long as he is alive, with "Imagination," which celebrates imagination as the only source of "wholeness." Such wholeness is celebrated in "Interior Events" by the wish for words so apt and for feeling so keen that the world and poetry will be one. If men would achieve this harmony, the poem says, they must recognize the paradox that the flesh—the individual and earthly—may be home to universals, and that the stars—the remote and cosmic—may offer the particular. Discovery of this "interinvolvement" is a principal component of the maturity represented by Eberhart's work printed in *Undercliff*.

VI *Giving Voice to Two Selves*: Collected Verse Plays

When Eberhart spoke of the verse drama which he and others wrote for the Poets' Theatre in the early 1950's, he said that "I've never felt since the excitement of a belief that it is necessary to life."[10] The upsurge, he said, was an "exciting social phenomenon," a "sociological mystery" which he cannot account for. Eberhart's own efforts in verse drama illustrate for the theater historian the difficulties of writing drama in an age which sees ambiguities rather than rights and wrongs. His plays are meditations on their topics—poetry to be read rather than dramas to be produced. Even his latest works are essentially nondramatic, although in them his stagecraft and his ability at writing dialogue greatly improve. The concern in this study is what relation the plays have to Eberhart's poetry: how they illustrate and perhaps contribute to his development as a poet, not what they may signify in the history of theater.

Eberhart considers the poem "Choosing a Monument" an early effort at drama.[11] Written in the 1930's and published in *Undercliff* in 1953, it was not included in *Collected Verse Plays* (1962). Another play written in the 1930's, "Triptych," appeared in *Poems New and Selected* in 1945 and again in *Burr Oaks* in 1947; it is included in *Plays*, but it has been discussed in the section on *Poems New and Selected* because it illustrates Eberhart's early position that there is a fairly sharp line between the spirit and the flesh. Eberhart says of his work in "Choosing a Monument" and "Triptych" that he did not get beyond "verse dialogue with three characters."

In one way or another, all the later plays present a contention between what *The Mad Musician* calls "the rebel ego," and a cautious, calmer, maturer self. The two selves seem, indeed, to represent two aspects of Eberhart. Still within him is the Romantic, immature, daring, exultant youth who seeks to pull down from the sky a "bravery" that is not accessible to him. Along with this characteristic, cautioning and sometimes opposing it, is the maturer voice, chastened by knowledge but willing to listen to the earlier voice; and, though sure that mystery reigns, it is too knowledgeable to merely exult, seeking, instead of "bravery," an understanding of self and circumstance.

These selves in turn may be related to the positions of Will and Psyche as Eberhart described them in a lecture at Johns Hopkins.[12] Will, he says, is of the body: it is active, makes something happen, is impure and "interested." Psyche is of or beyond the mind: it is spirit, is passive, makes nothing happen, is pure and "disinterested." Though Eberhart obviously prefers what he sees as the claims of Psyche, he does not dismiss Will entirely; and he accepts the idea that there is some involvement of the one in the other. In the plays, that is, a strong voice still speaks for writing that will declare inspirations, that will seek to achieve a fiery intensity, a bravery not held back by rules and logic. A voice not as fervid, but recognized as truth-telling, cautions against the egocentric and the heedless, urging attention to the world outside the self and to disciplined expression. The poet, of course, may listen to both voices and arrive at his own combinations.

The opposition of these two lines or threads is not absolute, and there is no sharp line between the value systems represented by the characters in the plays. Eberhart repeatedly has his characters comment on the inability of this era to create tragedy because it lacks the certainties of belief necessary for tragic experience. Men live today, he says, in an age of ambiguity in which they can produce only comedy.[13] He is careful to observe that by comedy he des not necessarily mean that which produces laughter. His comedies are observations and presentations of some aspects of what he sees as the human predicament.

In his stagecraft, he deliberately simplifies his characterizations, working for what Denis Donoghue labels "one-dimensional expressionism."[14] Thus, like Stephen Crane in *The Red Badge of Courage* and Ernest Hemingway in *A Farewell to Arms*, Eberhart often avoids given names for his characters; he prefers such labels as Author, Consulting Author, Professional Psychiatrist. Some names reappear in one play after another; and Eberhart explains that, since several of the plays may be pro-

duced in one evening, using the same names may help preserve
"consistency."[15] Interested in a universal human situation, he
also avoids individualizing the personages who appear in the
frames that he uses in most of his plays. Even the central
characters are simplified to represent a trait or a point of view,
for the interest resides in the ideas the characters represent,
rather than in flesh-and-blood complexities. Eberhart also takes
a step toward breaking down the division between actors and
audience; and, in his last plays, he begins to break down the
division between frame and central incident. The idea presumably is to involve the audience more closely with what
is happening on the stage—to engage the spectators at more
levels than the intellectual. Finally, there is a marked development in Eberhart's use of dialogue. The lines in the Preambles
are good poetry, without necessary relation to an action. By
the time of *Devils and Angels,* and especially *The Mad Musician,*
his lines are so closely involved with the action that they could
not stand alone as poetry, but they give much better support
for the action.

Three of the pieces given in *Plays* are short exercises in
dramatic writing. Eberhart says that he later came to see that
plot is the essence of drama, that *Preamble I* and *Preamble II*
are exercises in "somewhat Shavian" dialogue, meant to precede
a full action, to be "strong intellectual fare for a hardy audience."[16] They are scarcely as intellectually difficult as Eberhart
seems to think them, nor do they possess much Shavian wit.
They are, however, good poetry because their verse is vivid,
changeable, and clearly expressed; and, especially in *Preamble
II*, the poetry conveys ideas without being smothered by them.

Preamble I brings Poet, a character much like Eberhart
himself, into confrontation with Author, a would-be guide
who attempts to calm his flights of fancy, to discipline his
mind and imagination, and to turn his interest outward. Poet
wants to be a "world-protagonist," to be dramatic because he
feels that "There is still something to be exaggerated." He
thinks that his poetry has not reached some of the depths he
wishes to probe, that perhaps he has been too egocentric.
Author agrees that Poet needs a "cause," that he has been too
flighty, and that he should be "society's nerve ends." He invites
Poet to deal with the comic, gives trite advice, and suggests
that to be merely free would be to stagnate. By this point, indeed,
Author is becoming an increasingly unsympathetic character.
Poet is reluctant, feeling that to turn to disciplined consideration

of social issues would cool his fire because his intensity depends on his "savage selfhood."

In a passage that is perhaps the best poetry of a play that is well written throughout, he talks of his poetic realizations of Death, which resulted in a "purging," and of Love, which brought him recognition of "nurture," "solace," and "purpose." These are real achievements, and Author dismisses them too easily. But Poet is swayed, seeing himself as having been led by "illusion" and saying that he will "admit I never came to grips with life." Author knows, of course, that Poet has indeed done well; but he continues to urge him to sign an agreement to renounce individuality and to do his bidding. He even attempts bribery, offering fame and women. He cleverly admits to being "a sort of Devil," then says that he is also something of an angel (but informs the audience in an aside that he has no influence with angels). Still reluctant, Poet agrees to follow Author, who, while "faking a Sign of the Cross," now orders him to renounce his past habits and declares that he has become Everyman. The play seems a paradigm of Eberhart's own considerations on the problem of whether to turn from the emotional individualism of his early work to recognition of "flesh."

Preamble II is more directly concerned with specific problems of a playwright. The character Author here resembles Poet of *Preamble I* in his determination to write, but he also has taken on some of the practicality urged by the character Author in that play. In *Preamble II*, Author is talking over his plans to write drama with Consulting Author (C.A., for short). C.A. is something of a scholar, a university man who is perhaps too fond of verbal amusements and esoteric study to suit academic officialdom. Author asks his advice, though apparently his aim is as much to have a sounding board as it is to obtain ready answers to difficult problems of judgment and taste. Author says that he wants to write a "gigantic" tragedy, an aim that C.A. quickly regards as grandiose. He suggests writing a comedy, and Author agrees because he sees that this age lacks the "belief" on which tragedy would have to be based. Conversation about days at Cambridge includes recognition that, when young, they never realized that society "determined us"—that what seemed their joyous freedom was actually made possible by the economic system. Author speculates on the possibility of a play that would do away with action to give pure thought. But, remembering that he wants to know truth and himself, he recalls the serious achievement of his own poetry, the realizations of Death and Love that Poet talked about in *Preamble I.*

The dialogue then turns to a consideration of several necessary decisions. Author and C.A. discuss the use of various characters or stories—Job, Freud and Jung, Oedipus, Christ, conscientious objectors (whose wartime conduct evokes some of the play's most vigorous verse). They come to no conclusion but begin to talk of love as subject matter in a passage in which Author, as in *Preamble I,* speaks of being a Devil; but this topic slips away in delighted recollection of a girl both men knew when they were young. When they discuss possible choices of writing style, Author at first suggests "fluid and florid" writing; C.A. holds out for discipline. Author thinks that he might use an "amalgam" of styles, and that in any case he will write in an American manner. Before C.A. leaves, Author remembers that he has wanted to think of style as a matter not of merely verbal choices but as an expression of "all you've known and felt," of the whole man. C.A. warns him against too much near-religious dedication and a tendency to be "oracular." He advises that the "wise" do not attempt too much but see what the world is and "make the best of it."

There is so much of Eberhart in both characters that one feels, as with *Preamble I,* that what one really has is a dialogue between two selves of Eberhart—that though Poet in *Preamble I* and Author in *Preamble II* most directly represent him, there is also some of him in Author of *Preamble I* and much of him in C.A. of *Preamble II.* Since the second Preamble does not create a sharp opposition between its two leading characters, it thereby accepts the ambiguities and ambivalences that Eberhart believes are representative of human existence. The Preambles are thoughtful considerations of problems facing one beginning a career as a dramatist; but Eberhart, who recognizes their weakness, says that they "were skirting the problem."[17] This problem, he adds, is "action, action and character inextricably welded."

One more exercise, *The Apparition,* preceded Eberhart's full-length plays. Produced in 1951 at the Poets' Theatre, it may have been written before either of the Preambles. Unlike them, it is a short play in itself rather than a dialogue about playwriting. It presents two characters in a central incident which is placed in a frame that introduces it and later comments on it. An amateur but serious group of actors meet one evening when all are tired and want to do a light piece, "spicy" and "frothy." Robin, the writer for the group, says that the evening's performance is a "little picture of an impish situation." He takes the role of John, describing him as "Everyman, the protagonist."

The incident opens with John, who is traveling on business, writing his wife a letter in his hotel room at midnight. Answering a knock at the door, he finds a young girl who comes in to talk a few minutes. She has been bored with her boyfriend and has come upstairs to choose a door to knock on in a spirit of adventure. She says that she has to decide soon whether to enter a nunnery. John makes an advance or two, which she fends off; one of her refusals includes a remark that she knows men are vile because she reads Robinson Jeffers. She decides that she will go south to think over her decision, and leaves somewhat quieted. John has enjoyed her visit, says a one-line prayer for her, and goes back to his letter. The girl, one takes it, has been the "lissome" apparition promised by Robin. The other members of the acting group now comment, with some mild ribaldry and many puns. They are about to go home when somehow their punning becomes rhyming and they move into "a kind of rhythmic dance," a unifying, unified ritual" in which they gather in a circle about Robin and engage in a "routine" that consists of exchanging nonsense statements, most of them rhyming, several punning. After a few minutes, Robin brings it all to an end by promising that on another occasion they will "search out man in his deceiving dance."

The playlet has only two real characters—the several people in the frame are not individualized—but it is an interesting experiment with more colloquial dialogue and more action than the Preambles. Although it is scarcely dramatic, it does attempt to use Eberhart's fondness for the incantatory in a stage production. The effect of the ritualized dancing is to draw the players and, hopefully, the audience together in the spell. Presumably, it might thus release or exorcise yearnings and guilts summoned up by the central incident. The words, however, give no meaning to guide players or audience. Denis Donoghue finds it a defect that, during the central incident, the girl talks about her boredom instead of exhibiting it in action.[18] One might say that the closing ritual suffers from the opposite defect: it is all action, without talk that would give it significance.

The most overtly dramatic of Eberhart's plays is *The Visionary Farms*, which draws heavily on experiences of the poet's family in the 1920's. The central figure, Ransome, is modeled on Cy Thompson, the embezzler whose stealing brought near ruin to the poet's father. Though the poet wants to disapprove, he finds that Ransome, as bad characters are wont to do, draws most of the interest. Emphasis on such a character would suggest criticism of the validity of American dreams; but Eberhart's purposes prove to be ambivalent.

The play again presents a central incident within a frame. Scene 1, and scenes 14 and 15, support and comment on the action of scenes 2 through 13, the heart of the play. As in *The Apparition*, the opening situation is that of a group of amateur actors discussing the prospective evening's performance; and, as in the earlier play, the characters in the frame all talk alike. It appears that they have not taken their assignments seriously since, as Consulting Author appears, they are explaining how studies and children have kept them from learning their lines. Consulting Author, who has been prepared for this eventuality, brings in a cast of young actors from the university. He then waves a wand over the adults, declaring that they are purged of the ordinary, that each is "a part of Everyman." The gesture is a good one for drawing the audience into the play. Consulting Author says that the play proper will open in the Congregational Church Sunday School in a midwestern small town in 1919, with Thompson Ransome presiding. The frame has alerted the audience that it is to be prepared for later comment on the action which will now occur.

The central action opens with Ransome giving a Polonius-like collection of moral platitudes to his class, advice and maxims that urge "good" individual behavior and also striving for success as a means of furthering "the American dream." He discolors a dollar in a trick that is convincing to the children. Afterward at the home of the Fahnstocks—patterned after Eberhart's own childhood home—the father, Adam Fahnstock, supports Ransome by advocating "Health, honesty, and hard work." Only one of the children suspects that Ransome's methods were not ethical. Adam's success as vice-president of a company is illustrated by his discussion of the family's new car, new silo, and cattle purchases. His wife, Vine, tries, not very strongly, to suggest caution. (It is probably not much of an oversimplification to suppose that, if the Fahnstocks are accurate portrayals of Eberhart's own parents, the competing romantic and cautious aspects of his character may come from this mild opposition between the father and the mother.) Roger Parker, president of the company, calls briefly. He and Adam praise Ransome's moneymaking abilities and, in rather stilted dialogue, talk confidently of the "greatness of America," a greatness of course identical with their own successful exploitation of opportunities. At the end of Scene 3, as often at scene endings, some of the women from the frame comment on the action. They marvel at the boldness of the entrepreneurs, but one suspects that the play will not continue to show success only.

Scenes 4, 5, and 6, concentrating on Ransome, are much more vigorous. He is shown spending large, even extravagant, sums to promote his chicken ranch, "The Visionary Farms." Just as he was not above a bit of trickery in Sunday school, so he cleverly improves the appearance of a prize rooster by bleaching its color and gluing on tail feathers. The hint is that the chickens somehow parallel the human beings of the play, for one hears insistently that something is destroying the birds from inside though Ransome's superconfidence leads him to assume that, with his money, he can buy exemption and be assured that there are "No death and destruction on The Visionary Farms." Back at his office, however, Ransome in a soliloquy shows that he feels guilty; that, since he first took five dollars from the company's funds, he has plunged deeper and deeper into thievery; and that he now feels trapped by destiny. He wonders how he could have deceived his friends, decides that he is victim of an evil that attacks from the inside, and says that he is in agony. This scene shows that Eberhart is not going to condemn Ransome and prepares for the ambivalence of the play's outcome.

The other thread in the coming catastrophe is the illness of Vine Fahnstock, revealed in Scene 7 even as her sons talk of their successes in school activities. That her illness will be fatal is shown in Scene 8, where Parker assures Fahnstock that he will do anything he can to help. The women from the frame continue to comment, preparing for additional trouble to come. The action begins to reach its climax in Scenes 9 and 10 with the entry of young Ted Parker in the family business. Talking with the barber, Ted is already a bit doubtful about Ransome's activities. The women who comment at the end of Scene 9 think that perhaps the barber is the wisest spectator of the town's boom, but one realizes that he too has been caught up in the fervor. In Scene 10, Ted has found irregularities in the company's books; and, hearing of this discovery, Ransome immediately admits that he has taken $1,187,000 from the company in eight years. An immigrant and his daughter in Scene 11 relate that Ransome is still so popular that the people of the town serenaded him in jail and tried to raise bail money for him, a public attitude familiar to all who read newspaper accounts of embezzlements.

The father reaffirms the morality that revelation of Ransome's deceit might have shattered, remarking that Ransome for his pains has received a fifteen-year sentence to the penitentiary, caused his wife's death, and lost his name and honor. In Scene 12, Parker completes the financial catastrophe for Fahnstock by demanding that he turn in his stock in the company; when Fahnstock says that such behavior is obscene, Parker tells him that he has been assuming authority he does not have. The women from the frame comment not in the moralistic way one might expect, but philosophically: one says that all the characters have pulled the house down on their heads; another, who rather admires Ransome, thinks that it would have been better if his crime had not been revealed. One is being given further evidence that the author sees ambivalence in the action. In Scene 13, Adam Fahnstock tells his children of Ransome's crime and Parker's treachery, and then he reveals to them that their mother is dying. He indicates that, though she does not talk of it, she probably knows that death is coming.

The main action suggests not a basic unreality in the value system under which the people live but only an important loophole in it, a possibility for large-scale violation and corruption. The secondary action shows the destiny of pain and death for one who presumably lives an upright life. As one would expect from the presence of the frame that began with the opening scene, from Eberhart's way of ending such poems as "The Groundhog" and "The Fury of Aerial Bombardment," and from the several speeches in the play that indicate that Ransome feels guilty and that he is not to be condemned, the poet turns now not to solutions or conclusions to the issues the action has raised but to what are essentially meditations on them.

In Scene 14, Consulting Author, reminding the audience that these are not the times for Elizabethan violence, brings the concern back to thought, and he rejects the suggestion that "fidelity to action" requires physical activity. The reality of the times, he and others observe, is such that Ransome does not see himself as an Iago, that he will not escape from the penitentiary, and that Fahnstock and Parker are too complex to adopt the simplicities of violence. By the end of the scene, the several indistinguishable characters of the frame are agreeing that life could not be tied up in a neat dramatic package, that men are both good and evil, and that men in "modernistic, small society" substitute ideas for passions. Robin Everyman sums it up by hinting that justice will come with time.

But the play is not to end quite this dispassionately. The author himself breaks in to open Scene 15 (added in the Seattle production, to complete the characterization of Ransome); and he asserts that he objects to "all this fiddle," that he felt deeply about the characters, and that the play has failed to achieve more than "approximation." Consulting Author says the audience did not need the author's interruption, since the play is "of everyman." But, he adds, the play began a momentum that caused people to want an additional glimpse of Ransome. A scene within the scene follows, showing Ransome, after eight years in the penitentiary, refusing parole because he has become so involved in improving the finances and operations of the institution. Returning to the frame, all speculate in a final passage on the unknown future of Ransome after he has finished his sentence. Robin says that Ransome seems to have become a myth of the society that forged him, "real and brassy as itself." And Consuulting Author says that everyone in town recognized the sin of all in Ransome and that they sought, by forgetting him, to win redemption from that sin. Robin ends it by speaking this time not of justice but of truth: there is, he says, "a truth beyond character that is time."

Eberhart's ambivalent attitude toward Ransome—his awareness of the complexities of which he has some characters in the play speak—keeps him from making the play a strong attack on the values that the actions and character of Ransome seemingly question. Eberhart, indeed, appears like the townspeople: he recognizes Ransome's guilt but admires some of his enterprise. This characteristic makes the play more of a meditation on issues than a dramatic contention with a definite resolution. As the discussions of the characters in the frame indicate, Eberhart was, of course, much aware of such considerations; and to his credit, he did not sacrifice awareness of complexity in order to produce stronger stagecraft. One way out might have been more complex language and characterizations.

In a chapter on this play, Denis Donoghue quite rightly dismisses Selden Rodman's description of it as "a study in fourteen scenes of the collapse of a business empire."[19] But in rejecting the idea that the play is such a study, Donoghue reads it as a dramatization of the poet's "impression of the inevitable conclusion of the cult of Progress." However, one finds that the author is in fact ambivalent about progress, that he recognizes the deceit and hypocrisy of Ransome and the hypocrisy of Parker, but that he also withholds condemnation and, indeed, suggests that complexities not explainable in this life may lead to an understanding that differs from what the audience might now conclude to be the truth about all the characters. Eberhart's conclusions, that is, are not "inevitable"; nor do they strongly condemn the ideal of progress. In observing what he calls the "one-dimensional expressionism" in the characterizations, Donoghue recognizes the deliberate simplification Eberhart practices which makes the play less forceful, less dramatic. Eberhart has his characters comment that these are not the times for the resolutely dramatic, but one might speculate rather that Eberhart is more at home with lyric and meditative poetry than with dramatic action.[20]

Eberhart, in discussing his next play, *Devils and Angels,* again defends lack of a dramatic conflict. This age, he holds, is one of changing values in which men lack bases for judgments; therefore, one cannot write tragedy. One gathers that Eberhart would also hold that these times do not support firmly plotted comedy. He says that he conceived of *Devils and Angels* as a "presentation from a disinterested motive of the folly of man caught in the inescapable human predicament."[21] That is, he wrote simply to illustrate, without making judgments or arriving at resolutions. This attitude, he says again, is more suited to the present age because, though it lacks the bases for the tragic, it can imagine the comic in which Psyche upholds truth despite the Will of man.[22]

This aim is carried out in *Devils and Angels* by invention of a series of scenes which contrast with, mock, or reinforce each other; the point is that an ultimate destiny controls the characters. Author, in a somewhat pretentious opening speech, recognizes this control, and he finds it apparent as his ponderings are interrupted by a call for him to tend a sick baby. He discusses making a play about a pair of lovers, then is drawn into a wrestling bout with the Devil. He has been too sophisticated to believe in the Devil, but he accepts the assertions that his visitor is intimately a part of all human activity and of man himself. Soon after, Angel enters; he at first seems impossibly remote but reminds Author that, since men possess some measure of the intelligence that angels exemplify, they are somewhat angelic. Angel says that he has been with Author at those moments when Author has felt moments of visionary radiance. His message now is that Author must avoid being a "painful dogmatic absolutist," must not be lost either in awareness of evil or in dreams of the ineffable. He is to remember that there are mysteries beyond mind, truths beyond intellect. Angel, one deduces, represents Psyche, just as Devil is, at least in part, Will. Angel says finally that man was meant to know in his flesh the sublimity of the spiritual, to experience a yearning toward that which is beyond him.

Before Author can deliver solemn pronouncements on the visitations, however, he is interrupted again: first by his wife demanding his attentions to the home (which brings on a brief, humorous exchange about the manipulations of faculty wives), and then by a "member of the audience" who comes on stage to demand that the play begin. When "M.A." begins to be caught up in Author's rhythms, he is himself led away by his sweetheart; and Author comments that women always lead men back to reality. He is beginning a serious conversation with Consulting Author when there is another interruption, this one a "hysterical" and "vicious" scene in which two men argue over a government appointment (one might suspect that there is a connection with the delay in Eberhart's own appointment as Consultant in Poetry at the Library of Congress, a position first offered to him in 1951).

Consulting Author says that, in thinking about this incident, one must remember that everyone has some good and some evil. Author says that one must not be soft, that evil is profound, but he agrees with his wife that a deeper mystery is the advice of Christ to turn the other cheek. The serious conversation continues, with opinions that truth lies in the ego of man, that men somehow love the Devil. At this point, the Devil rushes on stage with a baby he says he intends to bring up properly. He sneers at the discussion, saying that he infiltrates the Psyche itself; and Author says that the "confused spectacle" they have been witnessing probably represents the truth. But Angel reappears to say that men must not credit the Devil with all power. Author and Consulting Author declare that men seem to be controlled by Devils and Angels.

One notes how Eberhart's dialogue has improved. The Preambles are good poetry for a reader, rather than dialogue supporting action. The talk in *The Visionary Farms* is often artificial; but in *Devils and Angels* Eberhart's intentions are very much in control of his language, with the result that there are no set pieces and little staginess: the dialogue is closely related to the action. But, although Eberhart has fulfilled his intention of presenting a series of scenes that illustrate the control of man by powers outside himself, he has again produced a meditation rather than a drama.

The Mad Musician is also essentially a set of scenes intended to illustrate a situation: the existence of "the rebel ego." It resorts once again to the device of a frame around a central action. A group of nonprofessionals interested in drama gather in the home of the Everymans to see a performance that will be put on by six young actors in addition to Robin, the author, who will himself take the leading role as Son. From the introductory dialogue, one learns that the production is intended to signify revolt against both the commercialism of professional theater and the errors of the "little theaters."

The central action gives a series of Inner Scenes and a set of Choruses. Son opens with a soliloquy telling of his objections to the intellectualism that interferes with his desire to be a composer. (The speech is the poem "Speech of a Protagonist" from *Burr Oaks.* As a poem, it was a recital by a frustrated poet; in the play, Eberhart has altered the opening lines to make it fit the musician.) After a passage in which personages from the frame converse about a glass of water, the scene continues with a near tableau in which Son's parents and his schoolmaster object to his proposed marriage to a lower-class girl and advise him to "renounce the sky," to give up dreams. College Psychiatrist and Professional Psychiatrist come on stage in turn; they too think that Son must be argued out of his visions of a career as a composer, and the professional promises to help Mother prevent the marriage.

The second Inner Scene is another soliloquy by Son. Again he criticizes stultifying intellectuals and declares his "rage" for music. Inner Scene 3 takes place three months later on Christmas Day. Mother complains to Professional Psychiatrist that Son has locked himself in his room after being in an automobile accident which injured his girl. The psychiatrist promises to have the young man put in an institution. A set of four Choruses now relate that the father is not so intellectual as Son, that he does not understand the youth's audacity, and that his mother is vain. Chorus IV is critical of the other Choruses as ineffectual, but Chorus I returns to give universal perspective on the matter by observing that each of the main characters—Father, Mother, Son, and Professional Psychiatrist —thinks that he is doing right and that all wrong inheres in someone else; and Chorus II says no one is sufficiently subtle and disinterested—that fate is in control. More criticism of intellectuals, especially of university professors, is followed by renewed comments by persons from the frame. Some of them find the play to lack motivation and to be too closely imitative of the life of a composer, Pendleton. Robin asks that they withhold judgment until the play is ended.

Son, who begins Inner Scene 4 with another soliloquy, now declares that, though others think him mad, he is in fact sane and that he plays tricks on the psychiatrist. He sees nearly everyone as hypocritical or as falsely ambitious, not only his parents, but also all of his college associates. Walking off the stage, he says that he must do "Justice." There now appear two graduate students whose conversation makes one realize that Son has "exorcized his devils" by striking, though not killing, his father. One student remarks that Son suffers the troubles of civilization—a divided mind. Persons from the frame question the dramatic use of the two young men, and Robin explains that he thought it better in a mind-bound age to have Son's striking of his father take place off stage. When one says that a comedy is supposed to make the spectator laugh, Robin replies that "The point's to show the folly of the world."

Two years pass, and the time is July 4. The fifth Inner Scene (misnumbered 6) shows Father and Mother telling Professional Psychiatrist that Son has married suddenly and become a Vedantist. The sixth Inner Scene (misnumbered 7) takes place another two years later, on a July 4 during World War II. Conversation between Father and Mother reveals that Son has been sentenced to four years in prison as a conscientious objector (an event that reminds one of the discussion of plots in *Preamble I*).

At this point, the inner play is abruptly over; and Robin says, somewhat ironically, that this is the "end of our first erogenous effort." Characters of the frame compliment him. One asks whether Son's turn to Vedantism and his marriage are logically probable, and whether it might not have been better to have him become a Catholic. Another suggests that Son might have been made a homosexual. Robin turns away such questions on the grounds that life has complications and that some possible solutions are too conventional. He ends the passage with the suggestion that the play may best end as it does, fading "into the quotidian." He says that he will invent a "robust, artful" ending. But two policemen enter, accompanying the composer Pendleton who declares that the play is libelous. Robin says that the action is not about Pendleton but about "every man," that it is "a symbol of the struggle of any artist." But the police and Pendleton are insistent, and they arrest and take Robin away as the curtain falls. The objection by Pendleton on logical but irrelevant grounds is a capstone to the play's suggestion that the "rebel ego" is the proper study: the ego of Son, of course, but also the ego of Robin, who has indeed modeled his play on Pendleton, and the ego of Pendleton, who, apparently without seeing the play, has acted on the assumption that it is a calumny on him.

The Mad Musician takes a longer step toward the breaking down of the conventional separation of actors from audience that Eberhart has experimented with earlier. It also breaks down even the separation of frame from central incident. Rare in Eberhart's work is the play's obvious sexual imagery. The introductory dialogue mentions an incident in which an eight-year-old girl painted a five-year-old boy's name on his penis. The suggestion is perhaps that the youngest generation is already starting to label others, to categorize and hence confine by attacking the most vulnerable spot.

In reviewing the six post-1930's pieces in *Plays*, one finds that they may be described as three exercises, one full-length play, and two briefer sets of illustrative scenes. All are meditations, rather than dramas in the traditional sense of a conflict that has a resolution. All are comedies because, in Eberhart's view, his era is not capable of tragedy. And all deal with a dualism coming, Eberhart says, from "a basic split in the soul."[23] One may regard this dualism as representing two selves of Eberhart that in some ways parallel the energies the poet labels "Will" and "Psyche." In *Preamble I*, the opposition between the youthfully Romantic and the maturely cautious is obvious; in *Preamble II*, there is more involvement of the one with the other, but the split remains.

In *The Visionary Farms* Ransome represents in the commercial world qualities not very different from those of the young poet who heedlessly sought a "bravery" from the skies. But even Ransome is not condemned, and both *Devils and Angels* and *The Mad Musician* avoid pigeonholing into good and bad; the plays operate simply as presentations or studies of the interinvolvement of good and evil in experience. The plays parallel, therefore, Eberhart's poetry in their presentation of what is portrayed variously as a struggle, a dialogue, or a dialectic. Whether the contention is held to be between the desires of Will and the inspirations of Psyche, or between the flesh and the spirit, the dualism is essentially the same. In both the plays and the poetry, resolution of the dualities is achieved partly by surrendering to "mystery" and partly by recognizing an intervolvement that unites the two energies.

CHAPTER *4*

The Discovery of Interinvolvement

I *Assurance, Without Certainties*

THE pervasive theme of Eberhart's later poetry is assurance that, despite the certainty of death, man can win a measure of triumph in this world and will continue to exist in some form after his life on earth has ended. This assurance was, of course, voiced earlier; but it appears more frequently and more firmly in his later work. Expression of assurance takes several forms: It may be a declaration that ripeness is all, a readiness to accept destiny in the trust that destiny is not extinction. It may appear as an assertion that wisdom contains a knowledge man does not recognize, a spiritual element that originates from higher sources than man's mind. It comes sometimes in recognition of a unity in human generations, a confidence that past, present, and future are one. It may arise from vision of a unity or harmony in a universe beyond man's sphere. It can be found in recognition of an intelligence that watches man, a power that, though inscrutable, testifies by its existence to an order and purpose in the universe. At times, it is sensed as a cosmic love, and sometimes it is specifically Christian.

Assurance continues also to arise from perception of an inter-involvement of spirit and flesh. This perception may arise from meditation on the "rainscapes" of a summer afternoon; or it may come more transcendentally, as when the reader is told in "The Wisdom of Insecurity" that "The strangeness of the poet's dream/ Will set what is, not what seems."

For man in this life, Eberhart's ideal remains the state of creative tension or balance. The thoughtfully imaginative man will be like the sailor of "Moment of Equilibrium Among the Islands": aware that profound depths appear only to imagination, keeping in this life to the "essential" qualities of "buoyancy, delicacy, and strength." This philosophical man will see his fellow human beings as comic yet admirable, to be sympathized with, though perhaps only from afar, because of recognition that

113

all men share in destiny. He will be more than merely contemplative; indeed, he will struggle to live in spite of his realization that he will lose the fight. In this struggle he will, as in "Off Pemaquid," achieve a measure of grace, beauty, and courage. By means of art, he will achieve poise despite the contending pulls of the dualisms that besiege him. And always he will remain sure that ultimate answers to his questions are locked in mystery.

II   *Faith in Renewal*: Great Praises

A poem that had appeared in *Undercliff* provides the title for the volume *Great Praises* (1957). This collection prints forty-four poems, of which twenty-seven reappear in *Collected Poems*. One theme of *Great Praises* is expressed in "Cousin Florence," a poem inspired by a visit to Florence Eberhart Hammond. When dying at ninety, she handed the speaker a piece of the Parthenon; he rates her "noble acts" and "powerful character" as superior to even the greatest art. She represents, one assumes, human qualities that constitute some of the "great praises" the book speaks of.

Eberhart continues to find grounds for hope despite his recognition of mortality. Use of the sestina form in the poem entitled "Sestina" gives the piece a melodic cast that helps move the reader to the feeling of melancholy. Exploiting the theme that death is inevitable, the poem tells men that neither thought nor action nor speculation on Christ will avail them. The poem might be improved by dropping the sixth stanza's flat discussion of man's disregard for Scripture, but the discussion shows why the poem is melancholy rather than despairing: there is ground for hope, whether man recognizes it or not. In "'My Golden and My Fierce Assays,'" the speaker asserts that there is no basis for hope because his "will" has been defeated. But he turns to recognize that he lives in a "blind delight," in a world of promises that he takes on trust. In "Ur Burial," a Sumerian aristocrat's wife expresses complete certitude;[1] she will poison herself in order, she thinks, to join her late husband in a blissful life hereafter.

If Eberhart can favor a trusting acceptance, and sometimes deny the claims of "mind," he can also on occasion write intellectual verse packing complex philosophical or theological speculation into short space. "Seeing Is Deceiving" tells of one who, having speculated deeply for a year, would not allow himself to see "the rose," which is presumably a symbol of Christianity. The

Latinate diction of the first stanza mocks the man's excessive reliance on intellect, for he would accept neither the disorder of life nor the order given by an artist. Yet his own "inner eye" was deceiving him because it did not lead him to acceptance.

"Analogue of Unity in Multeity" shows the "multeity" of the world by contrasting the meditative man with a railroad-crossing keeper. Like Mithridates, the thinker has supped so full of death that he is its master or at least its peer. The crossing keeper, a man interested in the mundane world, is "necessary," a part of life also. The unity of the title is provided by "another eye" in the sky that looks on both men and, indifferent to their differences, is a "point of agate reference," a standard with which both may be compared. The suggestion is not that some power in· the universe is indifferent to man but that it is indifferent to the differences among men: it sets an unchanging standard that holds true regardless of men's individualities. Though a bit complex in thought, the poem is clear in expression, done with an ease and authority that make it more convincing than the somewhat tortuous "Seeing Is Deceiving."

An indifference that arises from an intense "purity" is observed in "Sea-Hawk," a poem that inevitably reminds the reader of Robinson Jeffers's work. As one would expect Jeffers to do, Eberhart exults in the "inhuman perfection" of the hawk. But Eberhart's observations are intended to present admiration for the "grandeur" of the "impersonal" he sees in the hawk, not a contemptuous or scolding criticism of man. Though he will not surrender his sense of reality, the poet permits himself to recognize the appeal of simple delights. Regret is the mood of "Sainte Anne de Beaupré," a poem drawing on sights observed at the Quebec shrine named in its title. Watching a religious procession, the poet—though the fact that he is not of the faith is indicated by his allusion to the ritual as a "spell"—finds that it is "a hurt" that the dream of the innocent marchers does not coincide with the truth of eternity. Sadness also is expressed in "Mediterranean Song," in which the speaker indicates that, when "low," he likes to recall the high spirits of his youthful rambles in the south of France and in Italy.

"To Evan" gives the pathos of the death of a relative's son (the boy was the first son of Eberhart's wife's brother). The poem is sufficiently disciplined in statement to avoid outright sentimentality. The speaker recalls his inability to "suspend" the child's dying or to comprehend its "secret." The poem's last line—"I pass away silently and see him no more"—is Whitmanesque, suggesting that since neither energy nor tears nor rage will serve to allay the boy's pain, the speaker can only be an observer. Grief is denied in "The Day-Bed," a poem which reminds one of Whitman because it finds in the coming of new generations a renewal that masters mortality. The speaker feels "brutalized" when he looks on the cot that a woman he loved died on twenty-seven years before. But he recognizes that a new generation has come, and he celebrates the use of the cot by two lovers who find on it harmony and joy. He exults in the arrival of a child who, unaware as yet of destiny, represents the "very future," the "bliss" of human renewal. The poem makes skillful use of the cot and its associations to advance the theme.

"Formative Mastership" states the conviction that only vision can bring men even a limited understanding. In this "instant/ Just beyond perception," one will be happy that he will never understand what masters him, that he can know it only as a breath of spirit that comes in moments of harmony with the universe. Because such instants do exist, man must not let evil overwhelm him, though he also must accept his destiny as "victim" of a "savage dance." A captive of doom, all man can do is talk out his feelings. Such a poem recognizes a disparity between the imagination, which can see rich possibility, and the flesh, which must undergo doom.

But Eberhart also explores unity of flesh and spirit. "The Hand and the Shadow" states that, when the poet reached philosophical heights, the hand—a symbol for the mind, the instrument of the flesh—penetrated shadow, a symbol for imagination and mystery. But "shadow" soon outleaped the gropings of "hand," as though it sought such new but natural forms as that exemplified by ripe grapes. The "shadow," indeed, became identified with grapes: the imagination took on a natural embodiment. But "hand" too leaped forward because, though it faced death, it also was a token of resurrection and thus brought a radiance of its own. Both "hand" and "shadow" ultimately are glorious, and ultimately both "are one." They differ, it would seem, only in being varying aspects of one underlying reality of glorious mystery. Unity is also the theme of "Words," a poem that finds a "total myth," a comprehension of both flesh and spirit, to be achieved when one deepens in understanding. The speaker says that, when young, he thought of words as exotic, as entirely separate from himself. He next came to respect words as dominant powers. Finally, they came to make up a fabric both esthetic and durable, and he knew that the "world-memory" of himself, whatever survived of his imagination and body, would be made up of words.

Neither trust nor vision can make for absolute certainty. Whether one survives or dies at a given moment, for instance, often is a matter of chance. In the poem "On a Squirrel Crossing a Road in Autumn, in New England," the speaker while driving down a highway is pleased by the purposefulness of a squirrel, by his entirely nonintellectual response to the orders of nature. The squirrel can act with a simplicity that seems beautiful to man, who, it is implied, is all too complex. This empathy with the squirrel suggests the analogy that, just as it is what the squirrel does not know of the world that makes him beautiful, so it is what man does not know of God that makes up "the visible poem of the world." The mystery of the world, one deduces, is the "poem" of it.

But, in the midst of this meditation, the speaker is jarred back to the road: "... Just missed him!" This ending suggests another analogy: like man, God operates as a driver; whether He runs one down or misses one may be a matter rather of chance than of intention. There is a touch of humor in the incongruity of taking a squirrel with such seriousness, a humor evident, for instance, in the speaker's description of his attitude at one stage as a "whirling squirrel-praise." Eberhart has made the point that there is humor of another order also. In a letter he remarks that the ending line may be taken to refer not only to missing the squirrel with his car but also to "the wit of the meaning that I 'just missed' the point of the poem, or all its points, that finality has not been stated. The poem itself may be a joke on oneself for trying to understand."[2] It may be that all man's speculation on significances for the event is off the mark in this mysterious universe he inhabits. The poem is a favorite, Eberhart says, with audiences at poetry readings.[3]

Somewhat like Emerson, Eberhart holds that the uses of the past are not to provide codes but to inspire. In "Centennial for Whitman" he explains carefully that he does not imitate the older poet's forms or stance but that he speaks to him rather as a fellow mortal. The Greek motto at the head of the poem implies as much by saying that Whitman is inimitable though, of course, he meets death as all men do. The poem reports a visionary moment the speaker experienced on an occasion when he felt at one with nature, an experience rather like some of Whitman's own mystical states. The poet repeats

that he will try to speak his own true self, not imitate Whitman.
He recalls how "knowledge of death" came to him, intruded
by its own "will." As a consequence, he wandered in "fateful
duality," aware of his fallen state and of the absence of redemption. Looking into the "heart of man," he finds evil which
would master him if he did not hold it off with a sense of the
comic. This evil has been made more powerful by new weapons
and by doubts that spawn, or rise from, new delusions. The
only way out is "love," and the speaker decides that what
Whitman can offer a modern man is the "force" and "rapture"
he spoke with. Slow moving and flat in its expression, the
poem in interpreting Whitman as a poet of cosmic love shows
Eberhart's fundamental optimism.

Cosmic intimations often come to Eberhart while he is on
or near the ocean. In "Soul," a spirit that is evanescent, almost
hesitant, seems to move in from the sea. The speaker is not
sure whether it is a universal spirit, the soul of an individual
self, or something of both. By the final stanzas, he is addressing
it as "Father of mankind" and vowing his determination to
remember always its "dark intuitive presence." The pull of
imagination even in mundane circumstances is recognized in
"Fables of the Moon," in which the speaker will keep an eye
on the skies while he walks in the business world. Though
economic realities keep him earthbound, he is scornful of the
world that regards it as "gratuitous" for one to think of a whip-
poorwill. "Salem" is a deftly humorous suggestion of what
an imaginative man might see in New England's famous town
of witchcraft. In "The Return," the speaker still marvels at
the mountain light that once seemed to bring him certainty.
But now, though on the one hand he is less sure of the intuition
light brings him, on the other he is more certain of his oneness
with the mountains. The poem "The Giantess" is simpler in
intention; for it suggests a mood of sullenness by picturing an
"encompassing" yellowed female figure who dominates the
speaker in a lassitude suggestive of hot barren lands that may
be parallel to sterile hopes. It lacks the vividness to give it the
impact the concept would seem capable of supporting.

Neither inspiration, meditation, nor imagination can bring
certainty. If the primary certitude is death, the next most sure
is renewal—the theme of the superb transcendental poem "The
Wisdom of Insecurity." Renewal takes several forms—physical,
in the chemistry that rebuilds "disintegration"; mental, in the
"memory" that brings back thought of a robin; artistic, as in

the poetic record of a fine moth. Citation of such instances leads to the central assertion that "nothing is destroyed" because everything finds its own particular truth in "the eternal mind." It follows that there is no escape from this universality: man, when he dies, does not leave existence but only becomes "some other shape"; all present-day men represent Adam's line. Rather like Thoreau in perceiving the shallowness of time, as in the ending of Chapter II of *Walden,* the poet claims to look not only at but also through the sensory, to perceive "through the fish to the fish-hook." There follows the Emersonian conclusion that not sensory observation but the poet's "dream" will "set what is, not what seems," that the imagination gives reality whereas the senses give only a false show. The poem is a good representation of the major argument of Eberhart's later poetic philosophy. It makes effective use of citations of particulars to ground its fundamentally transcendental message in the concrete: if men are to dismiss the senses in some ultimate realm, they must recognize that in this life the senses are their only available instruments.

The conclusion of "Sunday in October" is more tentative. The speaker wishes that, like a beekeeper with his bees, "Providence" could be trusted to leave men at least the minimum sustenance required for their continued existence. The poem uses the sort of everyday observation one identifies with Frost; but, instead of Frost's colloquial note and strong irony, one finds Eberhart's typical mixture of the laconic with deliberate artifice in diction and tone, and his usual relatively direct statement.

Relations between meditation and vision give rise to several poems. A mood in which nature and the body share a rich lassitude that is akin to that of meditative vision is given in "Summer Landscape." The poem presents details of a warm, still, summer day on a farm where the principal action is the flying of birds. "Only in the Dream" salutes the counterpart to such a mood, the philosophical functions of a "dream" which may be vision or even death. Redemption, fulfillment, and understanding can come only in such a dream, the speaker says. He adds that "loss" will bring the mystical understanding that constitutes "triumph." This speculation is unusual for Eberhart, who more often thinks that men can find no reason for tragic experience.

"Nothing but Change" tells of observers who took with philosophic calm the changes they observed, including the deaths of others they knew. But, when age began to weaken their own bodies, neither Plato, Christ, nor intellect proved sufficient to halt or explain "unanswerable" death. The only assurance is that, in some mystical way, all is a "roundness," a "poetry." The depth of such mystery is given artfully in "Thrush Song at Dawn," in which birds singing at dawn are like a subconscious voice, a "divinity" that inspires despite all barriers. The speaker relates with sensible directness that he "would not be a bird" but that he would bear in "some lost purity, beneath the mind" a realization of meanings his spirit finds implied by the song, meanings expressed by "magic tones" that one loves and does not have to "know," to have access to either physically or intellectually. The poem, a superb symbolic structure, moves beyond the concrete and without direct reference to it, but with enough implied parallelism to a concrete situation to keep it accessible.

The best of the seventeen poems in *Great Praises* that are omitted from *Collected Poems* is "Society of Friends," a humorous verse presentation of Joseph Conrad's *Heart of Darkness* theme with an ironic ending. Grandiose Latinate diction and descriptive lines suggesting the mock epic give a playful air to the picture of apes who aspire to high mysteries and of a "Nordic" man who, seeming godlike to them, puzzles and alarms them. One learns that the Nordic admires the sensuality of the apes but also recognizes the likelihood of harm from them; and he muses on a way to escape before they should abruptly decide to tear him apart. In their silliness and treachery the apes suggest man himself. Nothing by Eberhart is more reminiscent of Wallace Stevens's combination of the bizarre and the exotic than the first line of this poem's seventh stanza, which refers to the "Nordic" as "The man who poured oranges into a blackbird."

A similar use of irony in "The Roc" conveys the realization that even a higher order of being than man cannot evade the mysterious forces which reign in the universe. A roc that has outgrown the limitations of his species sees the strutting, failures, and fears of mankind and determines to bring wisdom to men. But he finds himself cut off from men by a turmoil in the earth. That the poet says that the roc then flies away "instinctively" suggests that the creature, despite its superhuman abilities, is itself dominated by the powers that also control men.

"Theme from Haydn" has four sections that are related by juxtaposition rather than by verbal logic. The form suggests musical composition appropriate to the presentation of a mysterious journey that leads to a Judgment Day scene, then to a day of storms, and finally to a closing set of exclamations over the emotions released by the imagined experience. "What the Senses Tell" is an unsatisfactory description of maturity as a time when what once seemed the enormous problems of flesh, mind, and soul have been replaced by recognition of simple universal grandeurs and by equally elemental love. Taken straightforwardly, the argument is unbelievable; and nothing in the poem suggests that it is to be taken as irony. "Independence and Resolution" begins well with seven stanzas that depict a time when the speaker is in imagination "underground"; he is having a vision of the world like that one who is dead, yet capable of imagining, might have. The poem becomes flatly declarative and questioning, however, as it moves to stanzas describing man in the world. "The Glance" is artificially poetic. Three poems are reminiscent of Emersonian philosophy: "The Rich Interior Life" honors minds that respond to upwellings from the heart; "Idols of Imagination" asks for ability to cast out dualism and to recognize unity in experience; and "Man Is God's Nature" finds "godhead" expressed in man himself.

In "The Advantage of the Outside," which has the homely cleverness of some of Frost's work, the speaker discusses the advantages of sitting "inside," associating with one's fellow men, and looking out from that circle of warmth. He decides, however, that he would rather be outside looking in—free to roam the universe through heaven and hell rather than narrowed to merely human ranges. "On Getting Used to the World," a prosaic account of how one learns of destiny, ends with an appeal to value the artist who at least shows the kind of world men imagine. "The Whole View" and "Cold Fall" give contrasting attitudes of old age: the first poem presents the calm, wise, and perhaps smug assurance of one who purports to comprehend all the stages of life and to find assurance of divinity; the second laments the coldness which its speaker finds inevitable as one realizes that life is passing.

Two spars for Eberhart's man to cling to in the seas of doubt are art and the soul. "Going to Class under Greek Statues" finds Attic sculpture more moving than a meeting with a would-be nymph; "Vast Light" says that, whatever the speaker's experiences may be, he finds assurance in thought of the soul, imprecise though his ideas of it necessarily are. Unity of men with Adam and hence with God himself is asserted in "Remember the

Source." Imitating the style of Christopher Marlowe's "The Passionate Shepherd to His Love," the speaker of the poem "To Helen, with a Playbill" contrasts himself, a man aged by life and led on by fear, with the idealized Helen who will come in innocence and "fend off" all knowledge, even death.

III   *A Confidence Aware of Doubts*: Collected Poems

In addition to 119 poems selected from earlier books, *Collected Poems* (1960) prints 51 pieces in its New Poems section. Besides verse on such favorite topics as the nature of reality, the paradoxes of existence, and the need for light, these poems include considerations of man's own nature, possible development, and significance in the universe. The New Poems section begins with two meditations on purposefulness. "The Voyage" tells of the sailor who tries proudly to move forward by use of sails alone, but finds himself borne back by the tide and, determined to move ahead, turns on his engine. Desire to achieve a goal, or at least to move forward, has outweighed pride in one's skill. The poem exemplifies Eberhart's ability to find the philosophical in the mundane and to maintain a tone which is sympathetic but not overly emotional; his view is too factual to be ironic, and anger or sentimentality would be out of place. In "Off Spectacle Island," man's purposefulness is compared with the artistry and the play of sea creatures which bring the observer a delight that arises partly from contrast with man's reasoned activities. These activities are described as reaching "for Folly from Pride's Light," giving a clever double meaning to coastal place names.

Both Christian and pagan values are saluted in "The Seasons" and "The Noble Man," poems which exhibit something of Eberhart's ideal for man. In "The Seasons," a turn to Christ comes after Eberhart again parallels man's development with the passage of years. The man is hardly aware of, and is not overfond of, the early spring and is uncertain as he casts his nets for fish. Two stanzas headed "Spring Man" actually show circumstances of high summer, a season when intellect and imagination are in recess because they are overpowered by sensory delights, by youthful exuberance. Two stanzas entitled "The Man of Summer" find this man moving into autumn which, as in "The Groundhog," parallels the maturity that brings knowledge of death. The last two stanzas bring "The Man of Autumn" into winter, a season best described in laughter because it highlights the ridiculousness of man's efforts. Yet man is finally admirable because, "illogical," he looks for joy even while caught in winter. He is sure of his place, has developed the idea of himself despite the absence of verification from outside the self, and chooses Christ eternally. It is as though man has created both selflhood and divinity by an act of will. The poem has the somewhat elliptical syntax that makes for occasional confusion of the reader; but the sacrifice of clarity is a means of achieving concision; and unconventional phrasings lead to novelty of impact.

The man of "The Seasons" has an ultimate nobility. In "The Noble Man," admirable qualities are brought out immediately by matching the man the poet chooses to "posit" with both the Olympic mountains (reminding one of Eberhart's stay in Seattle) and the Olympian ideal of Greece. This "possible" man incorporates both rage and poise, both tension and grace. He compares himself with the Olympics but is not overawed by them; he knows "his own reality" and has outlasted fear and pride to arrive at courage and at action in contemplation. Neither a cynic nor an ascetic, he practices an active love. Wholly in a contemplative yet active balance, he has a halo of perfection around his brow like the laurel of ancient Greek heroes. The poem suggests comparisons with Marianne Moore's "The Hero" and also with her poem "An Octopus."

Comparison with Wallace Stevens's "Anecdote of the Jar" is inevitable when one reads Eberhart's "The Forgotten Rock." Although the rock of the poem is real, one gathers that men do not see its reality. They feel awe before it and are led by sight of it to think of other worlds. The poet comments that this subjectivity is analogous to the way men perceive the world itself, not as it is but "as we are." The poem does not end, however, with this poetically logical rounding off. A final stanza remarks that the rock has a cave into which a hawk inadvertently flew and was instantly killed. The rock, one assumes, was there and real all the time, despite man's failure to see the actual reality of it. Like Stevens's jar, the rock brings an order. The point for Eberhart, at least, is that men forget the reality that underlies the order they choose to live by. The poem also emphasizes blueness, reminding one of Steven's use of the color to symbolize imagination; and one may also recall the frequent use of rock in the Bible to stand for reality and truth.

Contrasting the "pure release" of a Catholic funeral service with the order and "prim dryness" of a Protestant funeral, the poem "Attitudes" is an effective presentation in which the author makes no overt choice. A stronger choice of values is indicated in "An Old Fashioned American Businessman." The speaker, using the first person, reveals himself as one who worked with intelligent ruthlessness but now regrets that he spared no time for loving. The businessman could be an inhabitant of Edgar Lee Masters's Spoon River, but the poem does not achieve Masters's best, in part because its eighth line is a weak participial phrase.

Soldiering continues occasionally to provide a topic for Eberhart. In "A Young Greek, Killed in the Wars," one who is recalling the dead finds a melancholy realization that the light which the dead have lost is both a deceiver and a preserver, that the most the poet can do is keep memory of the dead alive. The poem's first stanza is reportorial, but moving, because of its specific detailing of circumstances; the remaining two stanzas are too abstract. The poem "A Soldier Rejects His Times Addressing His Contemporaries" is intended as bitter condemnation of man's forgetfulness but starts off too sentimentally and fails to take advantage of the suggestions of Anglo-Saxon form in its first two stanzas. Much better than either of these is "Protagonists," a poem contrasting three men with combat records—two of them have been killed, one has returned home to be lionized—with the conscientious objector who "took Christ seriously." Imprisoned, he is describable as a "literalist of the imagination" (a phrase borrowed from Marianne Moore's poem "Poetry"), one who acted upon his inspiration. One may recall the approving discussion or use of conscientious objection in the plays *Preamble I,* and *The Mad Musician,* respectively.

A nontheological Christianity, probably close to Eberhart's own moderate Episcopalianism, and the qualities of inspiration and imagination that are associated with it, are topics for four poems. " 'Blessed Are the Angels in Heaven' " urges that any "great singer" who may appear among men be allowed to voice his art, but asserts firmly that the heavens will not hear him. Indeed, "angels" do not comfort man but instead work to keep him bound to the earth. "Villanelle" expresses the wish that man may be redeemed of "the will to slay" that he exhibited in war, but the poem assures the reader (or the poet himself) that Christ is within him. The poem is in the traditional form that gives it its title. "Life as Visionary Spirit" recommends that man value the contemplative mood and trust only inspiration. This inspiration, according to the fine last stanza, can come through radiance on a rose—one of the traditional symbols of Christianity. One function of imagination and dream, "Fortune's Mist" says, is to bring order to understanding and thus prevent absolute annihilation by destiny. The ending says that such ordering is art that parallels the mind of the creator. The poem thus links explicitly the imagination, art, and God. It would be more important as a presentation of Eberhart's thought if it had the vividness to give it impact as poetry.

Eberhart has always had gaiety of spirit. This quality is marked in such a poem as "Yonder," expressing a fondness for America that extends even to a liking for its place names. "Autumnal" recognizes the difficulties of existence but finds charming compensations in such minutiae as ants, clouds, and styles. Its speaker concludes that, even in old age, there is enjoyment and that, though he will stay in this world while he can, he feels "bound" to love of "the unfound." Such expression is the function of the poet, one is told in "Sacrifice." The poet is elected to help his fellow men bear their lives; in an intoxicated gaiety of the senses, he provides a fiction "intellectual and sensual."

The Romantic concept of the poet as one intoxicated is not, of course, Eberhart's usual view; but the frequency of his pleading for inspiration suggests that he would like to feel intoxication more often. In "Lucubration," he expresses the doubts and despairs of heavy, rainy-day thoughts; but he is finally able to hope for some "resolution," for "Song's mastery upon the starlit tomb." "In After Time" begins with a moving description of the future and turns to statement of new possibilities, but it falters when Eberhart allows himself to express tritely the hope that, in the future, man will see "fullness grow, big with purpose"—a wish vague enough to mean almost anything. "A Testament" includes fine stanzas asserting the poet's dedication to things of the spirit: lack of direct interest in worldly affairs, he says, has allowed him "the purest hours." But the first stanza is badly weakened by the trite thought and sing-song meter of its fourth line's allusion to a realm "Where the final values play." And the unnecessarily cryptic expression of the poem's last two lines weakens the consistency of tone.

Playfulness is deft in "Request," a sprightly plea for Edith Sitwell to autograph a book. Playfulness is serious in purpose in

"Love Among the Ruins," a poem implying the need to keep one's moorings in this world. The speaker says that he was once invited to visit the Italian art critic Benedetto Croce, but he did not go because his attention was held by skies and landscapes and ruins, and by the appearance of love. The implication is that the poet prefers realities to the unworldly musings he associates with Croce. (Browning's poem, "Love Among the Ruins," contrasts the love of a man for a girl with the love of kings and soldiers for glory.)

In "Anima," the speaker muses excitedly and rather grimly on the contradictions and savageries of life; but he concludes that the "falsity" one finds in experience is in life itself—a result of one's mortality, of one's betrayal by time. The mysterious paradox is that God and nature, the powers that dominate man, make him want to live even though this means that "the part," the individual soul, must struggle against "the whole," the universal order. The ending line asserts that "Each time we take a breath it must be deep," a direction that reminds the reader that the anima is both the soul and the breath. An ultimate paradox is that, in taking the breath that sustains mortal life, man is taking in part of a universal spirit or substance. Men are mortal, yet part of the universe: the contradiction is inexplicable, a part of the mystery of existence. "Love Among the Ruins" reminds men of the need to be aware of their connections with this world; and "Anima" expresses their plight as beings who, though aware of a world beyond this one, are subject to the processes of nature. The only answer to the problems these circumstances raise is that of "The Supreme Authority of the Imagination." Men long for achievement they cannot make by will or intellect; only by imagination can they leap over the walls that limit them. "Aesthetic purity" is given by the rose bud, and

> A rose of Spring seen with an even eye
> Never betrayed the seer; he leaps the sight
> And stands within ineluctable dominions,
> Saved in some haven of a sheer delight.

Perception of the esthetic significance of the rose, the object of beauty (and surely also here a symbol of Christianity), will exalt the observer to heights not otherwise attainable.

The inversions and redoublings that make the syntax of "Perception as a Guided Missile" unique also function to suggest the wrought-up state of the speaker's mind, as do occasional seemingly nonsensical exclamations and the quirky employment of verbs as nouns. Imprisoned in four walls, whether a prisoner of the state or a monk in a cell, he imagines what he would see if he could move in any of the four directions; and he recalls a dead woman he loved. His near hysteria is controlled only by his reliance on Christ, suggested especially in the capitalized possessive pronoun of line 9 and the capitalized objective case pronoun of the ending line.

Assurance by suggestion of Christ is also found in "By the Stream," a poem making use of the artfully playful, melodic verse that Eberhart frequently employs in his later poems, both because he has learned to write verse in this way—almost, in this manner—with ease and because it is appropriate in expression of consolation. Outdoors, enjoying the New England spring, the speaker tries unsuccessfully to comprehend the world by means of "language," by means of his art. He resorts to dream and feels himself merging with his surroundings. As evening nears, he suddenly loses his ecstasy, only to find it replaced by "A glimpse of Love, and in the brake an unicorn." The deliberate medievalism of "in the brake" points up the fact that the reader is to take the unicorn to symbolize, as it sometimes did, Christ himself. The poet has left off intellect; and, resorting to dream, he has attained a sudden but convincing moment of vision.

The lesson of fifty years of life, "What Gives" says, is that love is the highest value. Fortified by this belief, the poet can welcome even time, the power that elsewhere he sees as the agent of death and, consequently, as man's enemy. In "Austere Poem," truth is said to be equal with love. Truth tells man of his mortality, but must be accepted; indeed, since it forces the speaker to hold close to one he loves, it serves the cause of love.

"The Oak" declares that a fortunate few who keep close to nature's mysterious essence find they can rejoice in this life. But they must not assume that they can attain unity with nature by use of the senses. The "indeterminate scents" they glean are not truths of the world exterior to themselves; for they themselves govern their perceptions. A more extended treatment of the theme is in the four-page poem "The Parker River."[4] Hearing of a man's suicide by walking into the river that flows to the sea sets the poet to pondering on how going "back" to the ocean is "the great symbol of original mystery." Possible reasons and meanings for suicide include "a final affirmation," a "spiritual unity," a recognition of defeat, and a mystical merging with time.

The poem moves to a series of statements by moon, wind, stars, night, dawn, and earth spirits, each giving its attitude toward or symbolic message for man—that he errs, that he should know secrets of "the realm of birth," that he is a being to be sympathized with, that immortality awaits him though he does not know it, and that all nature, including man, exists in a unity. The poem ends with the thought that men of the future will also have the choice to swim in the river or to let themselves be carried away by it. Though the passages purportedly spoken by natural elements and objects may strike the reader as somewhat silly, the two stanzas that end the poem give a controlled and moving presentation of possibilities.

Mortality is somewhat less frequently a theme in Eberhart's later poetry, perhaps because of his increasing confidence in the possibility that death is not the end of existence. But the subject can still lead him on occasion to write powerful, sad, but unsentimental poetry. In "The Lost Children," which presents the effect on an observer of the drowning of two children, the observer finds his mood on the day after the event to be cautious; indeed, one effect is that there seems so great a threat in the universe that one may be afraid to admit that he loves another lest such feeling mark him for extinction. Going to the scene, the observer expresses in a brief, prayerful lyric his wish for the souls of the children. He then sees again the "impersonal" river and leaves with the wish to "hold close" his love. The poem is emotionally convincing because one recognizes the truth of the feelings expressed and sees the unforced implication that the stream of time holds dangers for all of us. The diction and rhythm are artfully adjusted to the poem's contents, giving an appropriate sense of slowness and caution in the opening and ending, and of lyrical prayer in the fourth stanza.

The poem "A Commitment" lacks the clearness to succeed with its declaration that the speaker is dedicated to belief in the "spirit that hovers over the graves," a spirit that hovers too over the stars and in the heart. The poem lacks concreteness; and its fifth stanza, which is meant to be revelatory, becomes merely clever. "Apple Buds" is pathetic, a strong but uncontrolled assertion of the poet's feelings soon after the death of one he has loved. "Throwing the Apple," based on D. H. Lawrence's painting *Throwing Back the Apple,* shows Adam in the Garden "unaccountably" rising to fling an apple at Jehovah. Adam's action seemingly represents man's doomed but courageous defiance of the power that imposes labor and mortality on him. Eberhart drops the word "back" from the title, suggesting that Adam is not merely reacting to motion originated by God but is himself originating the action. Neither intellect nor ordinary emotions can bring answers to the problems mortality raises. In "Light from Above," one hears again that light brings the only ultimate assurance that man can attain. Whatever men do or learn is unimportant beside the faith in unity which comes in glimpses whose truth is validated by "pure visual belief," by recognition that the sky, far superior to man's powers, expresses the "fiat of a great assurance." Though the poem relies on assertion rather than on metaphor or concrete detail, the speaker's enthusiasm gives it impact.

In the more ordinary hours of life, one must consider such matters as the usefulness of Romantic and Realistic approaches. In "Hoot Owls" Eberhart recognizes the "enchanting" qualities that have caused owls' voices to be thought mysterious, but he finds that Realism about the owls' preying purposes debunks this Romanticism. Yet he cautions that men must go "beyond realism" to attain "the poetical." One realization that is more profound than either Romanticism or Realism will give is that man, like nature, is controlled, at least in large part, by patterns of necessity. "Tree Swallows" finds in birds' behavior a "necessity" that "like ours" is "purposeful." Man, the reader is reminded, can climb peaks to freedom, but he comes home like the swallow to take up his own "graces and duties." The necessity that directs man, that is, allows for some flexibility.

Recognition of fellowship as a creature whose actions are patterned causes the observer of "The Clam Diggers and Diggers of Sea Worms" to feel love for the men who work the tideflats. Seen from a distance, they appear at first to be almost static, to compose a tableau of mankind as they make "necessary tracks." The moment of meditation passing, they become again men making a living; but they continue to suggest a "dark core," a "sombre purpose," perhaps because of the honesty and dignity with which they bend to their task, and the poet feels a mute love for them. The speaker of "The Clam Diggers and Diggers of Sea Worms" has as much enthusiasm as the speaker of "Light from Above," and he gives a much more concrete situation. The result is that the poem communicates a sense of profound meditation.

Patterning in the form of ritual is shown in "A Ship Burning

and a Comet All in One Day," in which men gather to burn
a worn out boat, no doubt playfully but also with a sense that
some recognition of the craft's "grace and charm" is called
for. As they watch the ashes wash out to sea in the dark, they
see a comet with a star in its tail, suggesting that the spirit of
the boat, or qualities it represented, are now in the heavens.
Their expression by ritual has brought a symbolic answer, a
sign that an intelligent power exists beyond their sphere. Possibly
because one cannot wholly commit himself to deep feeling about
a boat, the poem, though artfully and clearly handled, seems less
profound than "The Clam Diggers and Diggers of Sea Worms."

Darker necessities and patterns are intimated in "Half-bent
Man," in which a campus trash picker seems to move with
"profound, heavy purpose." The poet recognizes that the aged,
doubtless uneducated man knows little of the world of learning
that he serves and to which the speaker himself belongs. But
what interests the speaker is not the man's differences from, but
his similarities to, the inhabitants of that world and to all other
men. The trash picker's "dark burdens" and his "bent, half-
seeing, weary attitude" give physical representation of what the
speaker asserts all men feel. Like the trash picker, all of them
glean "gems and scraps" from the unrecognized "magnificence"
that surrounds them; like him, all of them are bent in ignorance
and burdens, at least partly because they fail to see the truth
of the universe.

"The Clam Diggers and Diggers of Sea Worms" and "Half-bent
Man" are two of Eberhart's better poems, partly because his
speakers find convincing physical representations of ideas and
feelings. "Hard Structure of the World" is equally good poetry,
though in a quite different mode. In it an appropriately varied
selection of details from observation builds toward anecdotes
from history and legend that lead to the decision that the "hard
structure of the world" equals a "world structure of illusion."
What is important, one is reminded, is awareness that there
is more to the world than senses and lore can tell man: "There
is something unknown in knowing./ Unfaith is what keeps
faith going." The ordinary hours and experiences of life can
suggest significances beyond themselves, but men must remember that, for revelation of ultimate understanding, something
more is necessary.

Realization that the world is in part illusory, perhaps is a
trick time plays on man, is suggested in "At the Canoe Club,"

a poem interesting primarily because it shows the high respect, almost awe, that Eberhart had for Wallace Stevens. In "Spring Mountain Climb," the speaker is drawn while near a lake and a mountain to make a "rugged" climb toward where "the source sounded." He enters a realm of "visionary grace" wherein bird call and sky seem miraculous, a huge eye searches the world, and he feels that the hand of God has written mysteries. He knows himself to be a witness to spirit even as he is drawn back to the "endless" burden of human routine. The moment of vision is less complete than most, for the speaker comes away without hints of the assurance Eberhart's men usually attain in such experiences.

In "The Passage," an autobiographical account of the poet's own early career, he tells of the sense of glory in which he was reckless with talent. Observation of pain and death caused him to move into "dark hours" that began to fade when he found in language a path to "statements of the eye" and to expression of "holy fire" and "unity." Flight was difficult, however, because he found himself in a "palled society" sunk in materialism. But rescue came when, by a river in a wood, he picked up an old cup. Touching it brought him in contact with an invisible town and antique dancers, perhaps a scene like that on Keats's Grecian urn. His final act was to put the cup to his lips, a gesture that brought him a sense of renewal. The situation suggests comparison with Frost's poem "Directive."

Questions of style are considered in "The Garden God," a poem that makes effective, somewhat playful use of a statue-fountain that people have named Homer. The water flows in ever changing ways as wind and animals influence its course. The speaker finds that this changeability represents style, and matches his own varying human moods. Concern over the fountain's flow suggests also the "magical despair" one may feel over loss of inspiration. But the fountain shows the order of nature and represents the "multitudinous harmonies" of a summer day; in short, it exemplifies what an artistic style may accomplish. In "Equivalence of Gnats and Mice," two of the qualities that style have are shown to be ethical values. A pillar of gnats in graceful motion weaves a "major harmony," and the kind treatment of lost mice by a mower shows great "delicacy." The speaker hopes for harmony and delicacy among nature, men, and his poems. In linking style with ethics, the poem is similar to "Meditation Two."

Eberhart continues to see the attainment of certainty and peace as temporary and difficult. In "The Gods of Washington, D. C." his speaker finds that sight of the headquarters of authority along Constitution Avenue reminds him of questions about the existence of gods. Men need gods; and, he says, they ought to tell us whether they exist. The treatment is half humorous, for the speaker knows quite well that no orders of his will cause gods to reveal themselves; and he senses a ridiculousness in his demand. The poem "Birth and Death" locates the "fearsome place," the most difficult realm for men, in the "in between," the stage between depth and height, opposites that one may read as depression and vision. The speaker of "Ospreys in Cry" is also aware of two poles of experience, but he exults in the sense of being both victor and doomed, the seer and the seen. His spirit, it seems, is glad to find identity with the wild, free osprey; it feels, indeed a "fleshed exultance" in the bird's untamed beauty. The poem's enthusiasm has energy because one may visualize the wild bird; "Birth and Death" is less convincing, however, because its oppositions are only verbal.

The volume ends with reassertion of the importance of "light." Less exultant and more diffuse than such earlier poems as " 'Go to the Shine That's on a Tree,' " the poem "The Incomparable Light" says that the poet has seen "light" in such mundane areas as "the turbulence of growing up," the "meshes of meaning of women," "political action," and "sundry deaths." This listing, flat and without verve, keeps the poem at a prosaic level that is not elevated by additional descriptions of "light" as an "Agent of truth" and "radical of time," nor by assertions that it "tells our song" and is the only source of hope. The poem serves, however, to remind the reader that Eberhart can find experience and sensory observations useful, can at times recognize an interinvolvement of spirit and flesh, but never forgets the faith that ultimate understandings can come only by vision.

IV *Acceptance of Incongruities*: The Quarry

The Quarry (1964), which contains sixty-two poems, opens with "The Kite," a relatively long poem in six sections exploring man's situation by means of analogy to the flying of kites. Commitment to both emotion and technique is evident in the opening passage, "Sensitivity of the First Flight." The passage's careful detailing of the manner in which one learns to become an advanced practitioner of the art of kite flying helps suggest an importance for the hobby, but the next three sections add details and speculate on significances. In Section II, "Theory," the aptness of the kite as an emblem for man himself is apparent in the explanation that, though the kite's basic motion is directed by the wind, it nevertheless is so constructed with vane and rudder that it is able to alter, if not totally redirect, its course; it is thus within limits a free agent, indifferent to forces and acting as though there were order in the universe.

Yet one also knows that such a kite may be a target for gunnery practice, and this information suggests several sets of analogies. Eberhart says first that the kite is a "symbol" of man's relation to the universe, that the wind is God, and that the kite's sail is like the soul. Moreover, the seeming freedom of the device is illusory, since man controls it. But the poet also sees other possibilities. These include use of the kite as a shield from the sun, as a "mask of evil" that, one deduces, may serve to hide men from unwelcome truths. There are also analogies between the kite and man's wish to fly free. Section III, "The First Flight, and Later," is a prosaic account of how a beginner learns by experience to handle such kites. The section may be intended to give solidity, but the reader is likely to find it arid. Section IV, "The Wind as an Abstract God," comments that the wind determines whether the kite will rise or be smashed, that man's realization of his inability to lift the kite teaches him obedience to nature.

The last two sections, however, show that man is not entirely helpless. Section V, the most vivid of the poem, tells the story of how, by use of intelligence, a man frees a kite stuck on the roof of an old lady who objects to all trespassing. The suspense over whether the attempt will succeed gives verve even to the details about technique. The final section, "Aerialism," is exultant, moving from presentation of the joy the speaker takes in a day of kite flying at the beach to recognition that his relation to the kite is like his relation to reality and to nature: like the kite, these are only somewhat under his control; for man's existence appears like the kite to be "Riding on the winds of chance." There is resignation in this closing note, but the joyful tone suggests assurance that, though chance imperils

man, there is reason to expect something more than what his
senses show.

A simpler analogy begins "The Spider," finding that, like the
spider, men are caught in the grip of nature and therefore are
symbols of the seasons. Yet, the poem continues, from another
point of view the spider is not a mere victim: his web is
marvelous; his walk, proud. The spider shows, indeed, the
"real myth," the mysterious truth about man himself. There is
yet "another dimension" beyond what the spider can represent.
Viewing the extent of the sea, one is carried in mind to the
universe. The question then is whether one thinks more profoundly when focusing on the particular, the spider, or on the
oceanic grandeur of "parables of God." The poem moves artfully from clear statement of relatively simple thought to more
imaginative interpretation. The next-to-last line is particularly
notable, a successful effort to lift the expression to heights in
keeping with the universal profundity the ending is meant to
suggest: "Or deeper a day or dance or doom bestride." Rhythm
provides most of the meaning in the poem "Sea-Ruck," a rhythm
suggesting that the speaker is awash on ocean waves which he
perceives as representing a continual ebb and flow of human
life. The poem's attempt at incantatory conviction is weak because meaning is sacrificed to meter and sound.

The ultimate realization about the situation of man is given
in "The Place," a poem that wonderfully exemplifies the delightful playfulness Eberhart has learned to use for serious expression.
Typically, the playfulness arises from acceptance of the inevitable, from recognition of the incongruity of man's bold dreams
with the facts experience teaches him. The speaker reports
that one eventually finds there is no special environment for
the poetic, no never-never land of golden "Hullabaloo." Stanzas
2 and 3 in their talk of colors and transparency remind one of
such poems by Wallace Stevens as "Thirteen Ways of Looking
at a Blackbird." But the expression is Eberhart's own, as is
demonstrated by the mention in Stanza 4 of "energized/ Gods
and beings, rich purposes." America continues to be a place
of imperfection and paradox, not the artistic environment of
poets' dreams. The speaker recalls the search for a special
place, and he dares to jest at failure to discover such an Eden:
"Hello! Poetry Place." Neither psychology nor other routes
he took led to a special realm. He comes to realize that "En-
trenched, my flesh is/ Poetry's environment."

Man's situation, in short, is that he can by imagination obtain intimations of realities beyond his world; but he must expect to live his life within this world, subject to powers beyond his control and even to whims of chance. Eberhart's ability in the use of the playful to advance the serious is scarcely matched in twentieth-century American poetry. Wallace Stevens is no more profound and seldom is so clear and direct; E. E. Cummings's talent is limited chiefly to lighter poems and satire. Not "serious" but delightful is "Clocks," an eight-line remark on the marvel of a fairy figure who stepped out of a metal case.

The speaker in "The Hamlet Father" says that, if Hamlet had lived longer, he might have gained understanding equal to that of Shakespeare; and, consequently, he might have behaved in "a different fashion." The poem is unsatisfactory because its precise situation is not clearly envisioned. Clearness of thought is burlesqued in "Four Exposures," a macaronic poem in that it mixes precise statement and assertion with unexplained metaphor and unconnected (and deliberately disconnected) metaphor, puns, and exclamations. It is a fine hodgepodge that might be better if somewhat shorter. Toward the end it turns more serious, but its efforts at seriousness are either trite or flat.

Unity is the topic of "La Crosse at Ninety Miles an Hour." Making an automobile trip along the upper Mississippi River, the speaker at first prefers the rock, which—as often in the Bible—symbolizes spirit, to the river, which stands for time and the world. But he comes to realize that rock meets the same end as the river, and he finally feels that there is "Small division between the world and spirit." In "Impatience as a Gesture of Divine Will," the poet seems to mock the man who allows "fine revolutions of the mind" to keep him believing in individuality even though waves of spirit break over him. These waves at one and the same time give him the spirit that he believes to be unique, and demonstrate in their flowing the fundamental unity of all men. Impatience, perhaps to declare mistaken individuality, has ruled the man spoken of in the poem; he has failed to see what new evidence has shown—the unity of life. Thus, he may sit in terror to listen to "authority," as in church on Sunday, but escape in the evening by imagination to kinder realms. Imagination, paradoxically, can also conduct him to the mental "revolutions" that mislead him.

Unity between living and dead men is the theme of "Nexus," which finds the dead "hovering on the air" that surrounds men.

Everything he does, the speaker says, has "a backward length," a connection with the past; for the dead can "make and shape" events of the present. In "The Record," Eberhart's speaker foresees unity with the stars, a "victory" for the soul. The first six stanzas are somewhat inchoate because they rely too much on unexplained abstractions—"the soul's periptery," "the battle of being," "the ultimate cause." In the last three stanzas the speaker declares that he feels sure that he can ascend to a "higher light" where he will not be in the grip of dualism and will discover the origin and history—thus, one may deduce, the purposes—of the soul.

The poem "Contemplation" presents a brief summary of Eberhart's poetic philosophy. As such a description implies, it is more sermon than poem. The speaker feels himself to be a "naked man in sun light" who "lives to dance in his own imagination." There is no evidence that Eberhart, the poet who dares to confront abstractions, has thought through the implications of the eighth line, "Individuation is the way to the universal." The poem asserts moralisms about hate and malice as negative and about love as "an active principle of communion"; but these are only trite assertions because they are presented directly. The stars, finally, are said to be a "heavenly emblem," symbolic evidence that peace and harmony wait for man in some realm of the future. "Divorce" is a rather prosaic lament over separation of man from nature. "The Mother Part" uses a playful style filled with alliteration, obvious repetition, and clever phrasing—all intended to convey unhappiness at inability to learn "the mother part," to achieve expression of the urgencies that man's failure to recognize God and to love his fellow men drive the poet to. The poet resolves that he will speak in awareness of mystery, that he will express the "truth of loss," the evil of experience. This resolution is unconvincing because it comes too easily after the long presentation of difficulties.

Such poetry smacks too much of the mechanically rational which Eberhart wants to reject. Attempting less, but achieving more, are several of his poems inspired by observation of deaths. "Loss," dedicated to V. R. Lang,[5] is a movingly lyrical expression of wonder at the death of a woman he has loved. The only direct philosophizing is in the first two lines of the last stanza: "I do not know how to say no/ To time that goes in any case, . . ." And these lines contribute effectively to the sense of wonder the poem is communicating. "Examination of Psyche: Thoughts of Home" is somewhat less personal; indeed, its speaker is perplexed that imminent loss of a woman of ninety whose death draws near moves him as much as it does; for she is only a "shadowy reflection" of a woman he had loved more deeply who died a third of a century ago. Yet the elderly woman is beautiful, a "statement of life's harmony." The situation arouses his questions: is there, for example, a "splendor undreamed of by man?" Unable to answer, he will compose an "epiphany for the living" and for all men, a suggestion that something of spirit lies behind appearances. Less personal but equally moving is "The Project," in which a series of quickly noted details establishes that the time is that of "the pageant of the American summer." In the midst of this high season, boys find a decaying animal, and one yells "Help! Don't breathe it!" The poem is pleasant, even humorous in its presentation of sensory details and in its quoting of the child's innocently ignorant warning. But the poem is serious because one knows that summer and youth, like the animal, will come to decay.

Though there are no answers to the questions that death raises, a man must have a guide to action, a set of values and ideas he can live by. In "Matador," the sight of a dead bullfighter wakens the speaker to "the rich meaning of necessity," to the fundamental force of human destiny. He urges himself to be in spirit like the matador: to maintain pride by means of grace and skill even in the face of "the brutal adversary." One cannot win, but the impossibility of a bang does not mean that the only choice is a whimper.

Eberhart has admired many of his contemporaries. "To Auden on His Fiftieth" is a pleasant tribute to the Anglo-American writer, full of allusion to shared experiences. William Carlos Williams was one of the two older American poets Eberhart says that he knew well (the other was Wallace Stevens).[6] The poem "To Bill Williams" suggests that the New Jersey poet was more in line with tradition than he admitted to being.

Eberhart is sometimes at his best when he expresses an upwelling of ardent intensity. In "Prometheus," he cries out his rapture at light and color, exclaiming that in a world of such delights "Adoration is the only word." Reason and argument are put aside: perception of beauty is for the poet sufficient proof that a world of spirit exists, that its creations are beautiful, and that man's most valid response to it is "adoration." By "adoration" he means the love and worship one knows and expresses, not by reason, but by feeling. But meditation on the spiritual is not to lead one to forget his kinship with nature. In "Old Tom" the observer learns from cats that force and violence are part of the way of the world, that elegance is not compatible with necessary violence. Cats, moreover, exemplify a praiseworthy indifference to death. The cat, indeed, teaches men something of their own root nature. This nature, one learns in "The Seal," includes a cruelty that may match that of destiny itself. The deer of "A New England View: My Report" endangers the men who hunt him, since, if they fire at him, they may hit one of their fellows on the other side of the river the animal is swimming in. Like the deer, the men share the peril of the "animal kingdom."

Nature has secrets of "natural majesty" that can hearten men even in moments of failure, one learns in "Eagles." The great birds of the poem represent a "newly seen" power that can startle men into fresh realizations of the "source" of inspiration, perhaps of man himself. The poet sometimes senses a unity with all of nature. In "Rainscapes, Hydrangeas, Roses and Singing Birds," the lush scene of a Washington, D. C., afternoon is a splendor that causes him to sense an identity with it: he is, he says, the "proliferation of nature" that he senses. He would rather "be and sing" than intellectualize, and in the beauty of the sunset he feels a glow of "benediction," an assurance that his days have not been in vain.

Certainties remain far off, however. The speaker in "Kaire" meditates on the superior understanding of Sophocles, but he concludes that even the Greek would not be able to comprehend the distance of love and truth from men's grasp. In "Kaire" the lark and the ocean waves suggest an unstated reassurance. Nature is also a source of inspiration in "An Evaluation under a Pine Tree, Lying on Pine Needles." Somewhat like Whitman's learned astronomer, the poet found writing "the abstract of Heaven" to be spiritually wearying and turned to the forest to see "the pattern of the universe." Throughout the domestic and religious experiences of his life, he was conscious that there was more to be known. He knew "wonderment" again when he returned to the woods. At fifty, then, he found that he could pierce the heart of his reader. Thus, though suffering continues, there is cause for rejoicing; one should "Bend to the northwind, and to the pine song." The poem is a series of simply phrased assertions, persuading by calm thoughtfulness rather than by metaphor or vivid imagery.

Nature, of course, is not an entirely sufficient source for man's probings and inspiration. Climbing a southwestern mountain. the speaker in "The Height of Man" has risen above timberline, beyond the zone where bluebells can grow. He reflects that the Penitentes were said to kill nonbelievers who climbed so high. Assuming for the moment that he might be killed, he cries out a recognition that the bluebells seem analogous to man's own early life, equalling the memories that sustain one during the time before he must confront the fact of death. Man climbs higher than nature, one deduces, because he comes to knowledge of death.

Love, for Eberhart, is not a complete answer to the problems mortality raises. Like the Christianity with which he sometimes associates it, however, it is a partial answer and one of the best available. "The Struggle" is elliptical enough to seem almost a riddle, but terse expression gives it a force that almost makes up for lack of exact detail and vivid imagery. The man of the poem seeks to live despite the chaos he senses in existence. He hopes that everything will "Become what it is not," that mercy and love will become dominant. In "Later or Sooner" the poet finds that, though he ages, he cannot yet make final statements about fate. Unable to give clear comprehension, he can nevertheless make a declaration that is both an inspiration and a platform for esthetic endeavor: "When man rose up, he loved,/ And when he loved, he sang."

Determination to wait until love is "victor and conqueror" in the world sustains the writer of "The Lost," who declares that he writes for the sake of all the lost spirits of this world, the people who have been "broken" and "reviled." He will keep their memory alive until their sufferings have been redeemed by a triumph of love in every human being. The speaker of "The World Situation," who has fought to achieve redemption for his fellow men, discovered, when he set out to meet life, that men are evil, that his own heart, indeed, is evil. He battled without understanding, coming closest to comprehension when he relied on feeling. Redemption appeared finally in the form of a woman, representing love, who caused men to cease their struggles against each other. An allusion to Gethsemane gives the poem a suggestion of Christian feeling.

Eberhart may find delight, a value in itself, in simple physical

scenes and actions. "The Water-pipe," addressed to Bharati
Sarabhi, an Indian princess who visited Cambridge, Massachusetts, remarks with pleasure on the contrast between the
way she handled her own pipe and her manner of handling a
Western one. Although the implication is that the woman wanted
to keep her own culture uncontaminated, the point is to present
the wonder she aroused in the observer. The exuberance of
youth is recalled in "Hark Back" as the speaker, reflecting on
the esthetic pleasures of a visit to a museum, remembers experiences on a youthful bicycle trip. In such a poem as "Hardening
into Print," the poet, by describing his vigorous struggle to
find and express "immaculate joy," shows that this search has
been his aim. In "The Master Image," the poet quickly suggests
the failure of observed details to comprise an understanding;
then he asks whether communication with other men could
be achieved if they shared a view he once had of deer leaping
by a cliff at dusk. A "master image" would express the godlike
exuberance of "Hark Back" and the joy of "Hardening into
Print," but it would also express the unity that links men of
the past and present with those of the future. The hope in
"Looking at the Stars" is that young lovers in the future will
see the heavens not as a rationalistic century does but as the
poet himself did in his youth—as portents of elusive but wonderful meaning and as assurance that hope is valid.

Faith in such assurance gives quiet authority to the splendid
poem "May Evening." The speaker reflects that some man of
the future in a rapturous moment will realize the unity of all
times. The speaker senses his kinship, indeed his identity, with
men of the past, with all those who have known an "instant
of apprehension." He knows that he cannot remain long at
such a peak of comprehension, but a moment suffices to convince.
Delight fortifies hope most strongly in the lyrically exultant
"Vision," a poem that admits doubts but does not give in to
them and that, in the perfection of its execution, matches the
beauty it exclaims over. Two hummingbirds at the poet's study
window remind him of bells or children; the birds seem "sent,"
angelic messengers. When they come a second time, he cannot
see them as the "brown machines" his intellect tells him they
are, nor can he accept realism's suggestion that their life span
is limited to "The frail duration of a Flower" (the line is borrowed from Freneau's "The Wild Honeysuckle"). They are
for him "hummingbirds of hope" because they sum up the

categories of beauty. In so doing they sing for him, all through
his being, of "purity and power," of highest hopes and intuitions.
The clarity, control of tone, and carefully prepared move from
the concrete to the abstract all contribute to the poem's
excellence.

In "Ultimate Song," the poet hopes that the song of the
thrush, which seems to have significance for man, may remain
ambiguous and elusive. The poem deftly, and effectively, uses
a rhetoric pattern analogous to that of a rationalistic argument
to advance its fundamentally lyrical plea. There is no rationalistic explanation of the discovery the poet makes in "Moment
of Equilibrium Among the Islands," but he finds it importantly
hopeful. Setting out on the sea, men in a small boat are aware
of dangers; but they sail on to an island where they climb
to a quarry holding water that "refutes" the ocean, that represents something opposite to danger. The granite blocks holding
water suggest the "hardness and fantasy" of the world. Though
the men seem to have come with a sense of purpose, the
observation takes only a moment and they return to the sea,
whose waters quiet as they approach their home. The title,
as well as the fact that the poet devotes twenty-four lines to
the incident, suggests importance for the briefly noted central
experience: men live in a world that has both dangerous seas
and reassuring calms. A moment of equilibrium restores or
reinforces a wholeness that is not always discoverable in daily
life. One may compare Frost's "Directive," in which men are
urged to turn to a restorative contact with the past. Eberhart's
man will attain assurance by observing—feeling, rather—the
contrasting qualities of the world, by recognizing that, if the
world contains hardness (which may preserve as well as
endanger), it also contains fantasy, an imaginative capacity
which can lead to contact with spirit.

Exultation in vision and the achievement of assurance through
it recognize energies or powers superior to man. Occasionally,
Eberhart speaks of worship of such powers. By decorating their
tree, the children in "Christmas Tree" unconsciously perform
an act of reverence that shows them to be so in harmony with
power (Christian, in this instance) that they need not "climb
to confront divinity" because they are one with it. Similarly, the
girls' offer of flowers at a funeral in "The Gesture" shows profound
grace and mysterious understanding that the adult observer can
recognize but not explain. Adults may turn to more definitely

patterned worship, even to ritual. "Sea Burial from the Cruiser *Reve*" tells of the burial at sea of the ashes of a cousin. The poem's tone of meditative wonder suggests an importance beyond what is directly stated: one is to regard the ceremony as a salute by the survivors and as a new birth for the dead woman. The poem is another illustration of Eberhart's great ability at blending melodic lines with simple presentation of circumstance to create an effect of meditative wonder.

The search for the origin of wonder causes Eberhart's spokesmen variously to withdraw from, to meditate on, or to struggle with the world. In "The Inward Rock," his speaker has left the "marketplace," the world of human society, to become one with rock and time and to find "imaginative freedom." In "Flux," the speaker points to examples of fate's seemingly arbitrary workings in this world, only to conclude that "Enigma rules" and there is no certainty. The "poetry," the mystery of tragedy is never dead, the reader is told in "Am I My Neighbor's Keeper?" In fact, the persistence of tragedy keeps the poet musing on the mystery of human experience. Tragedy existed among the Greeks, but it also occurs on a New Hampshire farm. The speaker remarks that there is no solution to the problem tragedy raises: a murdered corpse, for example, represents the existence of a force in the universe one cannot understand; and it explains nothing. The title's alteration of the biblical "Am I my brother's keeper?" suggests, of course, that one is not his neighbor's keeper because he cannot do anything to preserve him from possible tragedy.[7] One who searches after truth is celebrated in "The Diver." A metaphysical searcher, as well as a plunger in the sea, the diver seeks like the poet "the source," the origin of wonder; like an artist, he would work out an image of the age and face perils to find "meaning." The first twenty-one lines of the twenty-four-line poem are one sentence, a feat of rhetoric that is useful because it helps speed the pace. If the rhyme is sometimes too easy, as in lines 12 and 16, the shift to the present tense in line 20 is purposeful. Spirit is cleverly and gracefully saluted in "To a Poet Who Has Had a Heart Attack," a tribute to Bink Noll, a former colleague of Eberhart's at Dartmouth.

The ultimate superiority of feeling to intellect is illustrated in "Dream Journey of the Head and Heart." Somewhat as though exploring the storms that Frost mentions in "Tree at My Window" as troubling his head, the poet goes into his own depths to see what he can discover. But he finds himself stripped, almost lost, and unable to save himself by "head." Saved by "heart," he returns to the world by dint of "grace," on "sufferance" of mankind. "Heart," or feeling, seems thus to be connected with religion and with love of men for one another. "Winter Kill" implies an analogy between the hunting of bears and the search of the poet for words to express vision. In the opening line one seems to be reading of poets, for one is told that "Word traps catch big bears in silence." But the rest of the first three stanzas talk of bear hunting, remarking on the hunter's "sudden pride" and the poet's wish that the animal might remain "noble on the mountain side." The last stanza shifts back to poets, or to their retrievements, "big bears" who are caught in "Word traps" when total meaning is sought. A poem may come to the heart from a forest hill of spirit; but, unlike the forest bear, it will never be totally caught, will remain "elusive." Feeling, spirit, will never be added to one's trophy case.

One form Eberhart uses more extensively in *The Quarry* than in previous volumes is the short poem of characterization. In some instances, these poems are monologues, self-descriptive or meditative rather than dramatic. Although there is some concession to the colloquial, their speech is essentially that of the poet rather than the language such men themselves would use. The speaker in "A New England Bachelor" is a self-satisfied cynic who talks after his death in the manner of a character from Edgar Lee Masters's *Spoon River Anthology*. The poem lacks, however, the contrast with another character and the revelatory incident that Masters frequently used. Instead, the speaker relates, quite undramatically, some of the facts about his life which may be clues to his character. He has neither cynicism nor skepticism about himself—indeed, his opening statement that "My death was arranged by special plans in Heaven" seems straightforward rather than ironic. Consequently, one cannot feel that his cynicism about life bites deeply.

Percy, the speaker of "A Maine Roustabout," claims to talk with the accent of an Elizabethan, a matter one cannot judge; in writing, at least, his language is that of an educated poet (he alludes to "the conglomerate shore," speaks of tourists as "richlings") rather than that of an odd-jobs man who left school at sixteen. Language rather more elegant than the man himself would have used is not, however, necessarily a fault. The poem gives a reasonably graphic picture of such a character since the attitudes he expresses are appropriate. "Ruby Daggett," based on a woman who worked in a Hanover, New Hampshire book-store, is a better poem because the poet himself does the speaking and thus is free to make comments and contrasts the character herself would not have made. Eberhart avoids the temptation to give her the homely wisdom that sentimentalizers of village life put in the mouths of such characters. Instead, the woman is limited; the world's activities, including its books, go on without even her vicarious participation; at most, "In ink she suspected a waft of sage." "The Lament of a New England Mother," a longer monologue, is spoken by a woman in a time of mental crisis; the death of her husband has left her in a mood to wel-come death and thus to think of suicide by means of a revolver (or, at least, to feel that she is herself a "revolver," one whirled about by forces of despair). The poem lacks impact because it depends too much on direct assertion, especially in its first fourteen lines.

The progression from youthful innocence to saddened maturity, recognized by Eberhart as early as *A Bravery of Earth*, is illustrated in the paired dialogues "Father and Son" and "Father and Daughter." The girl of "Father and Daughter," still a child, sees natural objects like the sun as real; but the father sees them as fuzzy and menacing because he knows that simplicities change tragically with passage of time, that innocence is ignor-ance. The boy of "Father and Son" is old enough to assert his young manhood. Though he does not dispute his father's obser-vations, he insists that he must meet his own challenges. "Father and Son" is given in a highly artificial patterning of repetitions that effectively suggest the almost ritualistic universality of such debates.

Experience of death gives rise to a range of poetic responses. Like "The Lost Children," the poem "Death by Drowning" is a warning about the indifference, and finality, of destiny. "Ways and Means" is a powerful declaration of its speaker's determina-tion to defy death, despite his realization that it will conquer him. He will fight while he can, and will, as a believer in Christ, love "with the love of a lamb." Until death takes him, he will use poetry as taunt and weapon against it, a poetry that will sing of immortality. The poem exemplifies the brave defiance that it proclaims. A more comprehensive set of prescriptions is given in "Meditation One." The speaker recognizes the "nonsense" of man's ignorances, the "fiction" that seems to dominate his body and mind, the "baffled clarity" of his learning. He reviews man's growth from childhood innocence to the knowledge of death that causes him to turn to God and Christ. But awareness of divinity does nothing to explain the enigmas of man's immediate existence. The New Englander of whom the poem speaks finds a "god in the underbrush"—Pan?—who leads him to use poetry for songs to God. But his role as worshiper and poet does not give him new knowledge. He must recognize that, since "we know little," man must "cultivate" the world he spends his life in and hold on to everything "in view"—to all that his senses and imaginations provide for him to cling to.

"Meditation One" is conversational; leading the reader along a fairly rational path to its conclusions, it contains good sense but is not very striking as poetry (even Eberhart cannot make verse of a line like "I in a baffled clarity of unassimilated absolutes"). The poem serves, however, to free the poet from the urgency of philosophizing when he turns in "Meditation Two" to a consideration of style. One of his favorites for reading from the platform, "Meditation Two" is a thoughtfully honed restatement of the view, especially prominent in Eberhart's maturity, that perfection is not an absolute, not a finality, but a balance or equilibrium between opposing forces. Style too is arrived at as "the perfection of a point of view," an achievement of years of struggle and meditation on doubts, insights, enigmas. It is the result or expression of a temporary triumph, like that of the experienced fisherman who knows that a fine July afternoon will not last. In such moments, "reality" would seem to be a style itself, to indicate an order in earth and heaven; but, like the sailor of July seas, one knows that moments of calm do not last, that knowledge of evil has locked man in "dualism" that creates an unending struggle between the apparently contending forces of "good and evil, flesh and spirit,/ Damnation and redemption."

One release—not a final solution—for the problem of dualism is art, inspired by "unity," by thought of "immortality." Art expresses the man, and is itself a "triumph of nature" despite the inevitability of death for the individual. Having established these assumptions, the poet can assert that he sings "the harmony of the instant of knowing," the visionary moment when dualism resolves into unity. He recognizes that it is "of myself mostly that I sing," for what he has to say is an expression of his own imagination and senses, not necessarily a set of universal and permanent absolutes. Through the uncertainties of life, he will hold to the principle that style, the result of a moment of insight, should itself contribute to insight, should " . . . amplify and refine man's poise/ Be an instrument as lucid as the best of his knowing." The poem has abstract passages, and even the sympathetic reader gulps at such diction as line 50's "ramifications of disparate phenomena." But the poem is a convincing assertion and testimony, a restatement of the moral that style is the man. It is presented with enthusiasm and clarity. Unlike "Meditation One," it incorporates a leavening of the concrete and illustrative that enables it to rise above mere assertion, to appeal to the imagination as well as to reason. It is, in fact, a wonderfully developed presentation of an esthetic position that Eberhart has earned by a long career of successful accomplishment.

V *A New Gathering:* Selected Poems 1930-1965

The next volume in this poet's remarkably productive career is, to give it its full title, *Richard Eberhart: Selected Poems 1930-1965* (1965). This presents 112 poems, 100 of them chosen from earlier volumes. The selection includes both such deservedly well known pieces as "The Groundhog," "The Horse Chestnut Tree," and "The Fury of Aerial Bombardment," and the more recent accomplishments "Meditation Two" and "May Evening."

The volume prints twelve poems that had not previously appeared in book form. Four of these deal with the passage of time, or the possibility of temporarily forgetting it. "The Face, the Axe, and Time" makes its realization clear in its first line: "We survive for a while, and then we die." Yet, even while men are aging, they feel free and have hope. The prettiness of the poem implies that experience is not unrelievedly tragic. "The Illusion of Eternity" shows that man can be happy despite his awareness of destiny, since fine October afternoons give him an assurance that suggests immortality. Similar feeling inspires "The Matin Pandemoniums," which finds "no echoes," no sense of the past and hence of fatality, among animals and birds. They sing and move with grace because they have no knowledge of death. Entranced by them, one may for a moment ask what anguish is all about, what deeper revelation there may be than the "rich morning calls" of the birds. "The Rush" similarly celebrates a moment of assurance, a time when one departs from "mind" to enter a dance in a "passional" world that will leave a dream, at least, of an instant of unity when reality itself med to symbolize immortality.

Evil, failure, and conviction of need for redemption are counter-parts of the wish for peace and immortality. In "The Killer," sub-titled "On the Assassination of President Kennedy," the assassin is the purported speaker who reflects after his own death on the hate, "evil will," "fate," and lack of love that caused him to shoot the President. The poem is too preachy to be a convincing presentation of Lee Harvey Oswald's psychology, but it demon-strates by implication some of Eberhart's own values. The way a man who seeks to avoid brutalities is trapped in them is illustrated in "At McSorley's Bar." The speaker at first felt aloof from the troubles of a fellow man, but he eventually recognized that the other man was identical with himself. When the other man came to complete debasement, unable to seek salvation of any sort, the speaker, despite his "empathy," could not raise him. The speaker is too much like the other man; perhaps uncon-sciously, he is too tightly bound by the same dark realizations.

"Fishing for Snakes" may be read simply as a conversational, slightly marveling account of what is a common enough barn-yard pastime, raking snakes out of a well. It may, of course, be considered as symbolic of a search for evil, of a delight in seeking out evil in order to send it on its way. Whatever the permutations of evil and the proper attitudes toward it, the ultimate answer for Eberhart is in Christianity. In "Ordeal," the speaker feels "enriched" by knowledge of death, having seen it strike a thou-sand others. Nevertheless, the thought that death will come to him seems to end all hope. Not even the wisdom, the valued equilibrium ("stasis") of Classical Greece can reassure men. For true evidence of something beyond the grave, a brilliance that holds promise, the poem says men must accept the Christian message. Reassurance and fears are both expressed, of course, by the artist. "Action and Poetry" celebrates the poet's power as one "against society"; the poet is interested not in acting but in contemplation of action: he feels intensely the brutalities of life but expresses deep belief and courage.

The best of the twelve new poems are two in which Eberhart gives situations that exemplify the beauty and profundity he speaks of finding in the world. "The Echoing Rocks" tells of a marvelous noontide when distant islands seemed to speak, to tumble, to laugh. Their sound brought the poet a rush of feeling, a sense that he was hearing the sirens who spoke to the Greeks, even a sound suggestive of harmony between himself and the prehuman forms that first rose from the seas. As the moment passes, he salutes it as having been one of "visionary, imaginary glory." Equally fine is "Off Pemaquid," another poem in which the poet speaks of sailing off the coast of New England. Here he sees both the peril of the ocean and the "strut," the bravery of the men who continue to sail though seas may rise. The voyage, perhaps a day's trip, becomes an abstract of life itself in the melodically powerful final stanza:

> And so we make to far, expected landfalls
> Long suffering the waves of chance,
> Rolling and standing to the sea bells' calls
> In ancient challenge, and in nimble dance
> Small man, great ocean hurled down heavy malls.

Though forces are mighty, man can for a time evade them, even triumph; and there is beauty as well as courage in his enterprise.

In "Tones of Spring," the poet asserts that there is reason in the world about men for their reassurance—that answers to enigmas lie here if only the poet could express them. The light of a spring evening and the cry of geese suggest possibilities. Man might succeed if only he could make permanent the light that is "incomparable" but quickly fades, the love that comes only to bow to fate. These qualities and values, together with ability to interpret "deeper tones" that arise from "strong imperfection," would enable the poet to "penetrate" the mystery, the "shadowy stage" of existence, and thus save mankind. The piece is a cry for understanding which, though it reports a failure, is a success as a poem because, despite some trite phrases and excessive Latinity, its coherent variety and litanylike vigor compel the reader to share the poet's overwhelming awareness of possibility. This possibility is not as yet attained; but it is not therefore unattainable.

VI *Early Energies:* Thirty One Sonnets

Thirty One Sonnets (1967) prints a series of love poems written, according to Joel Roache, in connection with Eberhart's long, once close friendship with Louise H. Hawkes.[8] The sonnets show youthful fondness for "artistic" diction ("smote") and Shakespearian beginnings ("How shall I . . . ". "Shall I compare him to . . . ") as well as for the Elizabethan theme of inability to take one's love. The exuberance of the poems is too often given by flat declaration and quirky syntax, rather than by vivid or original metaphor and imagery. One considerable virtue is a quickness of pace that suggests the poet may have been impatient with the constrictions of the form. This virtue Eberhart recognizes in "A Note to the Reader," which says that, though he wrote the sonnets about 1931, only in later years did he come to recognize "the uniqueness of their energy and passionate flow." The sonnets must be considered early exercises, rather than accomplished poetry.

VII *Renewing Themes:* Shifts of Being

Testimony to the productivity of Eberhart's mature years lies in the fact that he brought out fifty-five new poems in *Shifts of Being* (1968). Continuing to explore problems of style that he had raised in "Meditation Two," he wrote in the mid-1960's a number of poems about poetry, the poet, and the inspiration of art. "Words" uses careful repetition to reinforce its thoughtful declaration of the way words work on substance.[9] They do not reshape men's faces and hearts, for the forces that have molded them are too powerful to be destroyed. But words do break down old ways of perceiving. They help men to recognize kinship with ancestors, and they give new brightness to the world by enabling them to recognize the "splendor," the "child," and the love within them. Thus, words create a mansion in the "universal dark." One noting the association of words and poetry with diamond hardness in such poems as "Words" and "Why?" may recall Emerson's note that "the day of facts is a rock of diamonds . . . a fact is an Epiphany of God."[10] Eberhart hopes to use words bardically, to express inspiration, rather than like, for example, T. S. Eliot, who shows in Section V of "Burnt Norton" that he values precision and formal patterning.

In the poem "Extremity," the hardness Eberhart desires is located in a mean between impulses of the spirit and the devil. But more typical is the rhapsodic determination of " 'My Brains Are Slipping in the Fields of Eros.' " The poet, recognizing his own imperfection, declares that he is driven to voice the inexpressible despite the domination of science. A fine stanza contrasts the poet with the seeker of mere truth:

> I stand in my times as a snowflake
> Remarkable in its ability to perish,
> And as a song of the woodland thrush among pine trees,
> Exquisitely attuned to possibilities of eternity.

He will, indeed, declare the heart of man—the joy and love he dreams of for the future. The poem gives the poet a bardic role

not usual in Eberhart's earlier work, in which recognition of
tragic experience usually cautions the poet to limit his aims.
Among these late poems, indeed, Eberhart sometimes adopts
the traditional Neoplatonic idea of the poet as a madman. In
"The Rolling Eye," this idea is indicated principally by the title;
for the poem itself is a typical expression of the feeling that
one is shaped by hard experience that is mysterious in origin. In
"To the Mad Poets," the wisdom of the poet again is an ac-
quisition of difficult experience; but the poet is described vividly
as rushing forth like an Arab warrior who races out of his tent
to shoot off his gun in a moonlit "Fantasia."

Whitman, in "When Lilacs Last in the Dooryard Bloom'd," and
Frost, in "Come In," deal with the song of the thrush as an appeal
that perhaps represents the voice of death. In "Against the Wood
Thrush," Eberhart contrasts the purity of the thrush's song with
the corruption of our "Televised and jetted" age; and he asks,
almost playfully, how the thrush dares to sing in an era that has
tried to thrust it aside. The ending line suggests that perhaps
here too the song speaks of death, for one hears that men fear it.

Eberhart only occasionally comments on other poets in his
verse. "To Harriet Monroe" tells of his early admiration for the
famous editor of *Poetry,* then of differing with her over suggested
editing of his writing, and ends with the line "Later we made up
and she died." This seemingly anticlimatic juxtaposition of the
more or less ordinary with the fact of death suggests that "she
died" may mean that, although they reconciled their problem, his
admiration for her was ended. Two poems show admiration for
Yeats. The better of these is "The Wild Swans of Inverane,"
in which, as a turf fire glows in a cottage on a lake in the Yeats
country, the poet hears a storm blow up and is startled by the
wonder of seven wild swans who represent, as they might in a
poem by Yeats, a "union of reality and dream." The poem
"Thoor Ballylee" describes Eberhart's feelings during a visit
in 1965 to the tower in which the Irish poet often worked.
Eberhart found the building itself to be unimpressive and the
creek, the "great symbol of water," to be dried up. The inspiration
that fed Yeats seems almost gone, for the poem adds that the
remnants of the building, but not Yeat's words, will see "Another
nine hundred years of history." Yet this dismay is not final; for,
despite the diminishment suggested by the unprepossessing
appearance of the setting associated with Yeat's work, the speaker
finds that his blood "Floods in riches of the sensual." More

dismaying is the discovery in "Trying to Read Through My Writing" of a lost poem Eberhart had himself written on a grocery sack. When he finds that he can barely make out the words, he concludes that he does not want to wholly decipher what was "impure" anyway; and he takes the action that "years sinuous and final" have taught him: he throws the rediscovered poem in the stove. The feeling is that time will take poetry anyway, that if less than perfect it might best be consigned to immediate destruction.

The power of art to express wholeness—a unity that cleanses —is expressed actively by rhythm as well as working in "Marrakech," one of several poems drawing on sights of a trip that Eberhart made to Morocco. Rapturous dancing in the marketplace raises the heart of the observer, as the rising and descending, dance like rhythm of the poem moves the reader. Art can take man from the middle state, the somewhat precarious balance of ordinary life, to either depths or heights. In "An Open Gate," the speaker discovers that music takes him down to hell itself; and he "almost" wishes that he could stay there, feeling that an absolute, even a doomed certainty may be preferable to the "imperfections" of mortal life. The strongest tribute to the artist in this volume is in "The Vastness and Indifference of the World," a poem that compares the behavior of a cat with a chipmunk to the "dialogue" of human beings, the vastness of the world being such that it can contain both these activities.

The poet asks whether it mattered that he saved the chipmunk from the cat; it does certainly not seem to matter to other human beings since, meanwhile, a mother is talking seriously of manners to a daughter who would regard any hint that her troubles are comical as "dafter" than the behavior of the cat toward its intended victim. The chipmunk hobbles into the bushes, as indifferent to the poet who has saved him as he is toward the death that threatened him—and as the mother and daughter would be to suggestion that the affair of the animals had importance. What the poet has done amounts to obstruction of nature, he reflects; as a man, his "instinct" caused him to deal out what he conceives to be justice, rather than allow nature to operate in its usual way. Like the cat and the chipmunk, and the mother and the daughter, the adults at a cocktail party that evening are victims of their own ideas of what is significant and are ignorant of, indifferent to, the "real" import of the incident. This import is that the poet is, simply, a savior: by his "inter-

vention" he penetrates indifferences and replaces the blind
activity of mere force with justice. Operating thus "to save the
world," the poet is a redeemer. One must marvel at Eberhart's
ability to make an esthetically powerful whole from domestic
circumstance, to exemplify in the poem the unity of mundane
and spiritual for which he calls.

Not even the power of the poet, however, can explain the
"mystery" which hides the reasons—Eberhart assumes there
are reasons—for tragic experience, death, and man's ignorance
of what may happen after death. Whatever aims and values
may govern the operations of the universe are hidden from man.
"The Standards" says that man knows only that time dominates
him, that the response to his inquiry about realities is mystery.
In "The Come-on," indeed, men are urged to make a proud gesture of their ignorance, of their state of "deadlock." (The poem's
allusion to Homer is probably intended to suggest a Classic
importance for the action, and also to refer to the fountain
named Homer that is mentioned in the poem "May Evening").
The speaker in "The Ascent" thinks at first that, by climbing a
mountain, he has reached a place of "the sublime," a haven
where revelations must surely come. But, just as he would
enter a "chapel," a "bower of bliss" that seems to promise
enlightments, he feels himself faint; and, recognizing his human
limits, he returns to the oceanic "enigma" that is all a man can
attain. Experience of such failure prompts the decision of
"Gestures Rich in Purpose" that the best a man can do is to be
ready for whatever may come to him, that since no action can
bring revelation one must be humbly receptive.

Failure to achieve understanding does not doom man to futility.
As in "Why?," he can still ponder the lack of messages about
"what to believe"; as in "To the Field Mice," he can still recognize
an implied parallel between the relationship of mice to men,
and of men to God, and consequently see a kinship between
men and mice. He can still, as in "The Enigma," suggest by the
form of a poem the mystery that it is intended to present. Here
one does not know what "Mine" in lines 1, 7, and 13; "the
whirling" in line 5; and "They" in lines 10 and 17 refer to. The
poem seems to contrast the troubles, doubts, and, in some lines,
the loves of the man spoken of with those of other people. The
man rows away, as though across hell. Whatever drives him on,
"It" has to do with nightmare struggles, with willingness to
suffer, and with fruitless recollections of past possibilities. The

poem itself thus is partly enigmatic, a fine illustration of the problem of understanding that it suggests.

If man cannot achieve goodness, he can at least recognize badness. In "Evil," the bad is represented by one who supports the United States' endeavor in Vietnam, and the poem has a social relevance not common in Eberhart's writing. The poet speaks of entertaining evil, an apparent "king of the world" and "devil incarnate," who resembles the poet and his friends. The talk is of the war, which no one at the table protests; at the end, all drink a toast to "the glory of our state." But the poet, who sees the "bloat" of evil, tells the reader that, when evil speaks, it is with "My imaginary bullet through his throat." Courtesy has restrained the impulse to protest, but the poet at least has shown what, under other circumstances, he might do. The poem by its restraint makes a stronger protest than a more directly editorial attack might achieve. Courtesy also restrains the speaker of "The Explorer on Main Street," who listens as a "big-jawed" traveler tells lurid tales of cannibalism in the Arctic. The poet thinks to himself that there is more of the mystery of nature and psyche to explore on Main Street than in the wilderness, that the explorer's hard experiences show only man's elemental physical drives, whereas "struggles of the soul" may reveal some now hidden haven for the spirit.

Though one may regret the dualism that shows a world of the imagination distinct from the world of the senses, he will recognize that the imagined is sweeter than the sensed. In "Hill Dream of Youth, Thirty Years Later," the poet speaks of the view he had when young of a world wherein life, the world men make for themselves, is a "meadow of lies" through which runs the "river of sweetness" that represents imagination, mystery, and sometimes assurance. He finds no human beings who symbolize beauty, for man's dialogue with man is "prompted from the wings" by such managers as Satan. He dreams of himself as standing on a hill, happy in his intuition that there is a better world than that of appearances. One may suppose that Eberhart suggests these views as ones of his youth because, though they appeal to him, he feels in his maturity that such happiness is too easy, that imagination and dream may bring realizations that are hard.

The strength that comes to the poet in moments of "madness" is celebrated in "The Birth of the Spirit." Forced to madness by "desperation of the sense," he finds that he has the strength of ten, that he can see wholeness and glory, that he can make a "saving" rhyme. The consequence is vision in a birth of spirit, a redness of vitality. A permanence of spirit is suggested in "Refrains." Peering through the "temple" that is his body, man sees only a pure gloom that increases realization that he is unknown in this world and is ignorant of the next. Men come and go; but the "mind," some universal human impulse, endures to hear repetition of man's searchings. Repetition of experience also suggests the enduring in "A Wedding on Cape Rosier," in which the event is "another" marriage, a pleasantly routine happening. Though an intruding dog suggests the charm of this world, the onlookers sing in Christian "wisdom" of the vanishing of everything of the earth. Continuity of names and acquaintanceships in New England suggests both the duration and the brevity of human experience. The poet concludes that the human event is brief and that it makes no difference to the eternities. To sustain his spirit, man must look to greater permanences than this life offers.

In "The Mastery," man is told to aspire to knowledge of spirit, almost by an act of will, if he would escape becoming the victim of the tragedy and death of this world. He must begin by recognizing that the mysteries he cannot penetrate are in fact "intricate insight," symbols of "fair depositions," of promises that lie beyond his knowledge. Either man will believe that there are such promises, or nature will reduce him to nothingness. Indicative of a drive in man to bring order to nature is a farmer's Japanese garden. Construction of the garden indicates that the man wishes to match "duration," perhaps the span of his life, with time, the span of the universe. He chooses thus to "aspire to gardens of eternity," or he is overcome. The poem's impact is increased by the poet's linking its stanzas tightly, the last line of each stanza becoming the first line of the next.

One means of ordering the universe is expression of love. "New Love," a melodic poem, is more complex than it may first appear; for it depends in part on color symbolism. In afterlife, the speaker will delight at last in the understanding of this world—represented by green willow—that is denied him while alive. He will achieve this comprehension, paradoxically, by "White dream," an act of "white will." The whiteness indicates emptiness, a riddance of the problems that troubled the speaker when alive; of course, it also symbolizes purity, wholeness of comprehension. Beyond earthly life, man will never die; for he will live at metaphysical height of spirit. The naturalness, the absence of merely intellectual approach that characterizes the relationship of earthly lovers, is illustrated in "The Haystack" by picturing a boy and a girl who "understand" neither the energies that surge within them nor even the richness of the luck that gives them a fine fish.

The inexpressibility of a more spiritual love is celebrated in Section I of "Love Pieces." Love, the poem says, is a "poetry of the world" that climbs beyond words. Though this love can never "possess the whole meaning," perhaps because it is wordless, it shares in the radiancy it touches on; and, when one sees some of it embodied in human beings, one is struck by its "ravishment." But such love does not live, and Section II of "Love Pieces" calls for the "death of love." When love comes to a man, he lives in brightness and glory: he cannot think; he cannot find words; he is mastered by feeling. The poet would celebrate this "paradise of the senses," but the mind has only temporarily been put aside. It returns to "bring love down," to make one aware again of suffering and disorder. Thus fate blocks man's love, and the poet realizes that what he wants to celebrate is rather the death of such love. The implication is that the death of limited mortal love will make it possible to attain permanent love, a radiant state which will not be in the grip of time, perhaps will unite intelligence, expression, and spirit.

That life is the true state of death, that what men call dying is in truth a rebirth, is suggested in "'When Nature Lies Asleep.'" The winter of the earth makes the poet think of the parallel with his own being as it endures mortal life. The winter of his spirit will remain until a spring brings the "white dream of death," the event that will enable his passage to a state of pure being. The connection of death with beauty is declared in "'Whenever I See Beauty I See Death.'" Because a woman died at a time when she was beautiful, the poet says, he connects death with beauty; and, since death is everywhere, it follows that the beauty of death is universal. Associations of death stir realization of the difference between dream and doom in "The Tomb by the Sea with Cars Going By." The speaker sees the white colonnades of a tomb, a white mystery of man's fate that confronts blue waters suggestive of the oceanic universe. Children, young marvels, play on the grounds while traffic winds snakily over the roads, the combination of the marvelous and the serpentlike suggesting the days of men's lives. Children can expect "bounty" from the sea, the universe, but men see the time that carries them along toward the "blue distance" of destiny.

Whatever complexities and philosophies may develop as one meditates on death, the response to its sudden intervention is "pure despair," the reader is told in "To My Student, Killed in a Car Crash." Line 10 uses the banal phrasing of a popular song—"the times they are a-changing"—to suggest the student's youthful ignorance of time's tragic meaning. Eberhart's emphasis is on the nature of the response, not on any personal relationship with the student. The poet finds his own mortality intimated in "Looking Head On," a title suggesting both the awareness of self and the imagined confrontation with death that come as he looks at a sculptor's clay version of his head. Though his own head will not last as long as the clay one, he knows that, in the end, both will come to dust.

How death jolts even one who feels assured of continued life is portrayed by the speaker of "On Returning to a Lake in Spring," who records the assurance he felt on a day of high summer and then, abruptly, the fact that a month later one of the picnic party committed suicide. A warning like that of "The Lost Children" is given in "The Ides of March." After looking closely at the stones of a cemetery, the speaker finds that everything he knows is somehow bound up in the intimation his staring has given him. He concludes that the best part of love is "not to ask what is our ultimate end."

The poem "The Symbol" suggests that the most comprehensive view of the relation of death to man that one can attain during his mortal life is realization that, though men are in the grip of time, there exists somewhere a grander power, a certainty beyond their present reach. The speaker sees in the air an eye (hence a perceiver) that is majestically separate from man but directs him, flashes "the command of time." On earth, the talk of two lovers shows that they are aware of time's dominance, even though they do not understand it. The speaker, by the last stanza, is identical with the eye in the air; and he sees the lovers as children but observes that he rides "through life and death," that he will "interinanimate the air": the eye intimates by its existence that a power with purposes for man is immortal and, in some way unknown to man, is linked with him.

Like Robert Frost, Eberhart can find values illustrated in nature but remains sure that man's being is only partially identical with that of the flora and fauna. In "Lions Copulating," he praises, with suitable humor, the naturalness of great beasts in contrast with the "lucubration" of men who try intellectually to find empathy with the animal world. In "R. G. E."—the title is, of course, his own initials—Eberhart reports a boyhood determination to "understand," to win permanence by carving his initials in a tree. But the gesture failed. The tree felt shame, for it existed in natural "brotherhood" with the earth and needed no belief in permanence. The poet felt pain both because he had injured "perfection" and because he came to realize the truth that his "human will" could never be calm and treelike. Realization that man can never surpass some aspects of nature —and should not want to do so—is expressed in "Outwitting the Trees." The poem contrasts the unchanging naturalness of trees with the changeability of man—not that Eberhart would dispense with man's shifting intellectual, artistic, and political interests, but that he sees that man might envy the trees' serenity. Musing on the trees, he realizes that any desire for permanence man may perceive in them is something he imports. What matters is their lack of human vices and their expression of the perfection men feel but cannot voice. One cannot "outwit" the trees, for their existence is not on man's plane; but one can admire their representation of qualities men long for.

What matters finally is not nature or philosophies but assurance, some intimation that death is not the end of existence and that the radiance man can imagine has a source that he will eventually come into union with—that there is a controlling, ultimately loving purpose in what seem the harshly tragic experiences of human life. Assurance may be specifically Christian, as in "Recognition." It may arise from clinging to a chastened belief in immortality, as in "The Immortal Type." It may come, as in "Opulence," from delight in the richness of summer sunsets and human maturity. It may appear in brief interludes of calm realization, as in the drawing-room moments of "Memory," in the quiet period of "The Winds," or in the presunset mysticism of "Solace."

Assurance of a sort comes too in observation of persistent, courageous, or skillful behavior. "Cliff" tells of a man who fought to free the propeller shaft of a boat in a venture that was perhaps foolhardy but proved successful. "Ball Game" draws an analogy between a base runner and the course of a man's life, finding the player's dashes and retreats a dramatic symbol of all human activity. "Swiss New Year" reports how observation of youths' holiday high spirits drew adults, people who had "known death," to suspend their disbelief and accept for the moment the "elegance and praise" of life that the youths express.

Assurance may even come as a mysterious birth brought on neither by action of man nor by any impulse that could be described as inspiration. In "White Night of the Soul," it comes suddenly, with no suggestion of origin, when one has been drained of all thought and feeling, has entered a "neutral place of unknowing" that is beyond emotion, civilization, ethics, and divinity. The title and the poem itself show that the prelude to reinvigoration is not the Christian mystic's dark night. The concept of spiritual emptiness may remind one of the Zen Buddhist belief in the necessity of a void, but nothing in the poem seems to suggest that Eberhart is drawing on specifically Buddhist theology. His state of emptiness is equivalent to a state of readiness, a state in which one's spirit is wiped clean of encrustation, not in order that he may continue in unknowing forgetfulness, but that he may receive new being.

As a poet of wonder, a neo-Romantic impressed with the mysteries of existence, Eberhart often presents and comments on incongruity and lack of understanding. "Santa Claus in Oaxaca" gives the sensuous feeling of a Mexican plaza to heighten the strangeness of the sight of a man walking awkwardly through it in a Santa Claus costume. The poet suggests that perhaps Santa Claus is hastening toward the future. Since this suggestion follows a remark that the fierce Aztecs are gone but some, at least, of the gentle Zapotecs survive, one may suppose that the note is one of hope that the future may be more gentle than the present. The question of "Boston" is "What do we do with our old histories?" The poem rambles conversationally through a series of allusions and anecdotes, many of them from Eberhart's years as a preparatory-school teacher; these are intended to show the individuality that old Boston represented together with the heedless changes of newer decades, changes which seem to bury the "intimate past" of eccentricity and color. There is value in that past, one gathers; but, like the modern citizens of Boston, the poet cannot state it. He recalls that the streams—of inspiration, one deduces, as well as of the riverbeds—were clear in the Minnesota of his youth, but "psychic" in his time at Cambridge and Harvard. He cannot characterize what seems to him the muddied, more complex stream of life in Boston; but the attention he gives it suggests that he is sure it is significant. Perhaps the future is always heedless; perhaps the color and individualism of the past are still there: the poet does not decide.

An even more colorful, if less eccentrically individualistic scene, is that of "Mexico Phantasmagoria." Here, however, the significance of the timelessness, the mixture of race and cultures, of worships and recreations, is clear. The rich variety makes one wonder about "the value of individual will," makes the ultramodern man who is poised for flight into space realize that Mexico represents ".... man's passionate realization,/ The struggle of mankind for brotherhood."

The future Eberhart wants is indicated in "Sanders Theater," the 1967 Harvard Phi Beta Kappa poem. The poet recalls his attendance as a youth at sermons preached in the Sanders Theater and the emotions of fear and joy that racked him as he thought of time and death, yet also of man's "radiancy." These recollections lead him to ask whether man will bomb himself to death, whether space travel is anything more than man's attempt to evade problems on earth, whether man can escape mechanism only by turning to the psychedelic. The poet answers his questions by hailing the "source of spiritual unison," and by remarking that there is a "ritual" pattern which requires suffering and indecision in this life. Under these circumstances, he values old myths but demands a new American international spirit—a worldwide brotherhood of men who will love art. In that unity, the poet asserts, man will "exceed himself," will triumph over temptation and failure. These assurances, of course, are matters of belief, not of logical demonstration. The poet leaves the discussion as he entered it, aware that mystery lies at the heart of experience.

CHAPTER *5*

Recognition and Achievement

I *Energies and Reputation*

EBERHART has covered an astonishing distance in his development from the fervid but callow youth who demanded bravery from the skies to the tragic ironist who can observe in "Sanders Theater" that

> And now I know that imagination
> Is freedom and that poetry is praise,
> I cope with man and am consumed by time,
> God stains the glass at the back of the hall.

The "mystery" which still holds him is that based on the fundamental paradox that man is a being who is able to obtain messages of inspiration yet is himself entrapped in the flesh. Eberhart has been concerned with ideas of mystery and mortality, dualism and ambiguity, love and Christianity, time and man's kinship with the past and the future. But since he is a poet, not a philosopher or a theologian, these ideas have furnished him not with problems to be solved but with energies for poetry. He has learned that the instant of art, whether visionary exultation or alert contemplation, is brief—that one struggles most of the time in the toils of paradox. He has learned also that art can be not only a product of vision and meditation but also an instrument for achieving these states.

The artist may even be something of a savior, may be the inspiring bard of " 'My Brains Are Slipping in the Fields of Eros'" and the guardedly optimistic sage of "Sanders Theater." There is a presence, a perceiver in the universe outside ourselves; but men have no direct communication with it and except in inspired moments can have no knowledge of it. Since mystery covers the purposes of this presence for men, the height of achievement is the understanding that ripeness is all, a courageous and even beautiful readiness to accept what time

160

will bring, chastened by knowledge that men must go through the processes of death but reassured by the faith that immortality awaits them. Reassurance comes from this faith, as well as from delight in nature and in man's kinship with all the created world. It comes also from Christianity, love, and the state of readiness to receive new being. The possibility of achieving new being is itself evidence that there exists a spirit outside the self.

Recognition that this intellectual and esthetic lesson lies behind Eberhart's poetry does not, of course, imply that it is the whole of his accomplishment.[1] It has not yet, however, drawn the attention of any large number of serious critics—a fact that is not surprising when one observes how long it takes for most poets to become presences in critical studies, as well as in anthologies and classroom discussions. Eberhart's work began to receive more than passing attention in the 1940's, especially after publication of *Burr Oaks*. His poetry is printed in two well-known anthologies of the 1950's, John Ciardi's *Mid-Century American Poets* (1950) and George P. Elliott's *Fifteen Modern American Poets* (1956). Being in the generation that was neglected because of the dominance of T. S. Eliot, Eberhart had scarcely begun, however, to achieve prominence before he was suddenly being regarded as a voice from an era that was already passing: no work of his was included in either of the two paired (and contrasting) collections of post-modern poetry—*The New Poets of England and America* (1957)[2] and *The New American Poetry 1945-1960* (1960).[3] Eberhart is not even mentioned in Roy Harvey Pearce's *The Continuity of American Poetry* (1961); but neither are H. D., Robinson Jeffers, Stanley Kunitz, Howard Nemerov, or others who surely belong in a full study. There are only two mentions of Eberhart in Stephen Stepanchev's *American Poetry Since 1945* (1965).

But except in the case of Pearce's study—a work notable for its inclusions despite its oversights—these omissions are usually due to arbitrary rules on the age of contributors rather than to neglect. A pamphlet on Eberhart's work by Ralph Mills, Jr., is included in the Minnesota series on American writers.[4] Mills surveys Eberhart's development and favorite themes to conclude with praise for his ability to "embrace with equal ardor and sympathy the events of existence in the world and the revelations of the spirit."[5] In another appreciative study, a chapter in *Contemporary American Poetry* (1965), Mills praises Eberhart's art for its skill at creating meditation anchored in the concrete. Eberhart also gets respectful, though brief, attention in M. L. Rosenthal's *The Modern Poets* (1960).[6] As this is written, Joel H. Roache III is completing a study of Eberhart for Oxford University Press, one that draws on material Roache collected for his dissertation,[7] a biographical study tracing a development from rebellion and alienation to acceptance. The dissertation was the result of long study of Eberhart's work and close acquaintance with him; and, with his book, it is sure to remain basic to any full consideration of Eberhart's career. Bernard F. Engel, in his introduction to *The Achievement of Richard Eberhart* (1968), finds Eberhart to be a neo-Romantic, some of whose best poems arise from moments of exultation and others from active contemplation.

II *A Major American Poet*

Eberhart's distinctiveness is due partly to the fact that his esthetic origins may be traced to Blake and Wordsworth, even to Tennyson. He developed his talents and matured in his career without coming under direct influence from his American contemporaries, from either Pound and Eliot, or Williams and Moore and Stevens. Thus, Eberhart was not a participant in the "modern" poetry movement. Though he differs in most conceivable ways from Robinson Jeffers, he shares with the West Coast poet an independence from the mainstream of twentieth-century American poetry. What Jeffers achieved by geographical isolation, Eberhart fell into, so to speak, by being born half a generation or more later than the leaders of "modern" poetry and the New Criticism. A contemporary of Theodore Roethke and Stanley Kunitz, he belongs to a generation that did not follow Eliot and Pound in reexploring and reasserting tradition, nor Williams in rejecting it. Calm about the matter, Eberhart uses traditional forms to pursue his goals.

As a member of the post-modern generation, Eberhart is committed to no programs or platforms. His closest approach to commitment is wary acceptance of a nontheological Christianity. Like Stevens, he honors the imagination; and, like Yeats, he works for interpenetrations of the sensed and the inspired; and he values the ecstatic moment. But he does not share Stevens's rejection of traditional religion, nor Yeats's acceptance of the occult and the mythical. And he is more direct and boisterous, less symbolic and refined than either of these poets. If his acceptance of ambiguity and ambivalence makes him less able to advocate a firm poetic philosophy, it allows him a range of topics and approaches broader than either Yeats or Stevens could accommodate.

As a post-modern, Eberhart writes of the self; even his plays seem dialogues between selves of the poet, rather than characterizations of others. He has relations to all three of the movements that Stepanchev considers the most important currents of early twentieth-century verse—the active traditionalism of Robinson and Frost, the free-verse experimentation of the Imagists and others, and symbolism.[8] But his applications and combinations of these and other tendencies are individual. Like Thoreau, Eberhart has taken from the stream of time such advantages as it presents but has resisted being swept along by its current. One may agree with Peter L. Thorslev, Jr., who concludes one of the best essays on Eberhart's work to date by saying: "Among contemporary American poets who often seem either academic and a little tired, or else full of fire and wildly anti-intellectual, it is a pleasure to read a poet like Eberhart, who has . . . something of the virtues of both camps: a keen intelligence, but also a warm humanity and a genuine inspiration."[9]

Eberhart insists that evaluative criticism is the highest form.[10] An evaluation of his work must take into account the large number of fine poems he has written on a diversity of themes in a variety of manners. One thinks of "The Groundhog," one of the most influential poems of the last four decades; "The Fury of Aerial Bombardment," perhaps the best of American poems on World War II; "Seals, Terns, Time," a splendidly incantatory presentation; "May Evening," a movingly quiet meditation; "The Place," a poem whose gaiety of surface helps develop its geniunely profound realization; "Meditation Two" and "Sanders Theater," in which the pose of mature counselor helps give not tired moralism but hard-won wisdom.

Evaluation will not be entirely adulatory. It will take note of occasional excesses of diction, substitution of sentimental rhetoric for ideas, flatness of phrasing, and fondness for generalizations that are not always earned or even supported. Eberhart, moreover, takes risks, including the great risk of using direct statement and assertion. Like many of his virtues, his faults are ones to be expected in a poet whose aim often is to record

unprovable intimations and to create incantations and celebrations. But a poet is judged by his successes, not by his
failures. Eberhart succeeds—whether his materials are statement
and assertion, or commentary, meditations, or celebrations—
when his inspiration gives him the subtlety in technique and
the power of imagination to make his materials serve his poems.

What marks Eberhart as fundamentally different in this age
of uncertainty that verges on despair is that he is a man of
confidence. His assurance is based upon a faith in intimations
that is possible only for a man who is by nature an optimist.
Believing that there is a "something" for man beyond earthly
existence, he does not focus on the problems that interest the
majority of his peers. Convinced that earthly existence is all,
they typically take as subjects such matters as bourgeois crippling
of the artist or the tormented psyche or the loss of old faiths
or the illnesses of society. For Eberhart, in contrast, the one
great problem is the one finality—the fact of death. His peers
for the most part dismiss this as an event that means only the
cessation of existence and consequently has little significance
for the artist. Believing, in contrast, that "death is but a door,"
Eberhart looks for the spiritual even in the mortality that
appears to be nature's triumph over man. At times he draws
on Christian doctrine, but one may suppose that this is because
he finds it an ally in its insistence on the existence of a realm
beyond this earth; certainly he is not writing devotional poetry.

Many of Eberhart's peers see a disparity between their ideal
of what life, especially life for the artist, could be and the
actuality they experience. Eberhart too finds a disparity, the
disparity between experience in this world and the promises of
a superior existence that he is sure that he senses. This finding
is for him a cause not for despair but for celebration. Observing
in the poem "Dam Neck, Virginia" that beauty may appear
even in acts of barbarity, he is aroused to a recognition of the
"beautiful disrelation of the spiritual." Eberhart comprehends
fully the tragedy of death and the evil in experience. Though
social issues are not his primary subject, he takes note of them;
one may observe, for example, that in the poem "United 555"
(*Poetry* magazine; October, 1970) the poet's realization that
the view from an airplane is beautiful does not cause him to
approve of the pollution and waste that the flight extends.
Eberhart's faith that the "disrelation" between the spirit and
the flesh is "beautiful" is not simple-minded. It is rather a

conviction that on a profound level there is unity despite the appearance of dualism. Attempting to comprehend the mystery of this unity is Eberhart's esthetic effort.

One may share the hesitancy about use of the adjective "great" that Eberhart has said is characteristic of this generation.[11] But there can be no hesitancy in terming Eberhart a major poet of this era. The creator of such a large number of excitingly moving poems is sure to have important impact on the future of American poetry. The breadth of Eberhart's accomplishment suggests that the future will consider him as a great American celebratory and meditative poet.

Notes and References

Chapter One

1. Richard Eberhart, "Why I Say It in Verse," in Paul A. Jorgensen and Frederick B. Shroyer, eds., *A College Treasury*, III (New York, 1956), 413-14.

2. Richard Eberhart, "Notes on Poetry," in John Ciardi, ed., *Mid-Century American Poets* (New York, 1950), p. 225.

3. Jorgensen and Shroyer, p. 414.

4. Stanley Kunitz, ed., *Twentieth Century Authors*, First Supplement (New York, 1955), p. 297.

5. *Ibid.*

6. Richard Eberhart, "How I Write Poetry," in Howard Nemerov, ed., *Poets on Poetry* (New York, 1966), p. 39.

7. See especially William I. Thompson, "Collapsed Universe and Structured Poem: An Essay in Whiteheadian Criticism," *College English*, XXVIII (October, 1966), 25-39. Eberhart alludes to a parallel between his own dualisms and Blake's; see Jeffrey Marshall, "An Interview with Richard Eberhart," *The William and Mary Review*, II (Winter, 1964), 4.

8. Ciardi, p. 226.

9. Thompson, p. 26.

10. The visit, and the interviews with Eberhart, took place on March 23 and 24, 1966. Quotations and biographical facts are from these interviews unless otherwise identified.

11. Kunitz, p. 297.

12. Richard Eberhart, "Richard Eberhart Discusses Group of Young Poets on West Coast," *New York Times Book Review* VII (September 2, 1956), 4.

13. The Baker Library at Dartmouth sent me xeroxes of these. One may also see "Encounter and Letters," *Dartmouth College Library Bulletin* IV (December, 1961), 37.

14. The occasion described is the Lambda Iota Tau Lecture at the Modern Language Association meeting, December 27, 1968.

15. In a letter to me of October 22, 1970, Eberhart said that before writing "New Hampshire, February" he had not seen Edward Taylor's poem "Upon a Wasp Chilled with Cold," which begins with a report of a wasp's actions while becoming warmed by the sun. Eberhart said that he likes some of Taylor's phrasings but feels that "the archaic language stalls the poem."

16. Richard F. Bauerle, "Eberhart's 'Throwing the Apple,'" *Explicator* XXVII (November, 1968), Item no. 21.

Chapter Two

1. Eberhart told Jeffrey Marshall that in *A Bravery of Earth* he was "reliving, in my own way, his [Wordsworth's] spiritual growth as a young man." "An Interview with Richard Eberhart," p. 4.

2. Cited by John Ciardi in "How Does a Poem Mean?," in Herbert Barrows, *et al*, eds., *An Introduction to Literature* (Boston, 1959), p. 667.

3. In his Introduction to *Reading the Spirit*, p. 5, Michael Roberts suggests that the implacable may be analytical reasoning.

4. John Lincoln Sweeney, a student at Cambridge with Eberhart, is a "close friend" now retired from his position as curator of the poetry room in the Lamont Library at Harvard.

5. Marius Bewley, "Lines," *New York Review of Books*, V (March 31, 1966) p. 20.

6. For example, in comparing his work with that of Wallace Stevens, as in letters to me dated November 4, 1966; January 24, 1967; and January 25, 1967.

7. According to Joel H. Roache III, Eberhart used "Maia" as an affectionate name for Louise R. Hawkes, with whom he had a close if primarily epistolary relationship for several years. (*Richard Eberhart: A Poet in America 1904-1961*. Ph.D. dissertation, University of Pennsylvania, 1967, p. 82).

8. Interview with me in Hanover, New Hampshire, March 23, 1966.

9. Eberhart discusses the poem (referring to it as "The Critic" and mistakenly assuming that it appeared in *Reading the Spirit*) in "Will and Psyche in Poetry," Don Cameron Allen, ed., *The Moment of Poetry* (Baltimore, 1962), pp. 51-54.

10. Letter to me, October 9, 1968.

11. Charles C. Walcutt and J. E. Whitesell, eds., *The Explicator Cyclopedia*, I (Chicago, 1966), 93-94.

12. *Ibid.*, pp. 89-90.

Chapter Three

1. Joel Roache, Preface, pp. l-lxiv.

2. Although the date given in the book is 1944, Joel Roache in his bibliography corrects this to 1945.

3. For a prolonged discussion of the metrics of this poem, see Ciardi, in Barrows *et al*, *op. cit.*, pp. 994-1003.

4. Walter Lowenfels, ed., *Where Is Vietnam? American Poets Respond* (New York, 1967).

5. Interview with me, March 23, 1966.

6. The John Cornford mentioned in "Song," the son of a faculty couple at Cambridge, was a poet who was killed—"heroically," Eberhart says—in the Spanish Civil War. Eberhart did not know him but had read his poems.

7. The situation is reminiscent of that suggested in Blake's "Auguries of Innocence," in that work's line, "Hold Infinity in the palm of your hand."

8. Interview with me, March 23, 1966.

9. *An Herb Basket* (Cummington, Mass., 1950).

10. Interview with me, March 23, 1966.

11. *Collected Verse Plays* (Chapel Hill, N.C., 1962), p. viii.

12. Allen, *op. cit.*

13. *Ibid.*, p. xi; and compare Robin's speeches in Scene 1 of the play *The Visionary Farms*.

14. *The Third Voice* (Princeton, N.J., 1959), p. 225.

15. *Collected Verse Plays*, p. x.

16. *Ibid.*, p. ix.

17. *Ibid.*, p. x.

18. Donoghue, *op. cit.*, p. 195.

19. *Ibid.*, p. 224. Selden Rodman's discussion is in "The Poetry of Richard Eberhart," *Perspectives*, X (Winter, 1955), 40.

20. Donna Gerstenberger remarks that a difficulty for Eberhart, as well as for Archibald MacLeish and Djuna Barnes, is the lack of a tradition of verse drama in America. She comments briefly on Eberhart's linking of the dream of success with the dream of the good life as pastoral. See her "Three Verse Playwrights and the American Fifties," in William E. Taylor, ed., *Modern American Drama* (Deland, Florida, 1968).

21. *Collected Verse Plays*, p. xi.

22. *Ibid.*, p. xiv.

23. *Ibid.*, p. vii.

Chapter Four

1. A discussion of "Ur Burial" by Richard F. Bauerle, and Eberhart's reply to it, are given in Charles C. Walcutt and J. E. Whitesell, eds., *The Explicator Cyclopedia*, I (Chicago, 1966), 92-93.

2. Letter to me, October 12, 1966.

3. He gave this poem to Paul Engle and Joseph Langland, eds., for *Poet's Choice* (New York, 1966), a collection of poets' favorites from their own work.

4. The poem is dedicated to "F. R. K.," Frank R. Kitchell, "a grand man" who was a family friend of Mrs. Eberhart's parents. He disappeared in the Parker River (in Massachusetts) early one morning; his body was found several months later.

5. In a conversation on February 6, 1968, Eberhart expressed to me much admiration for Viola Lang, an actress and writer of verse dramas who was active in the Poets' Theatre but died young.

6. Interview with me, March 23, 1966.

7. Anthony Ostroff, ed., *The Contemporary Poet as Artist and Critic* (Boston, 1964), pp. 141-66, prints a discussion of "Am I My

Neighbor's Keeper?" and Eberhart's answer to it. The discussants are Louise Bogan, Philip Booth, and William Stafford.

8. See Roache, *op. cit.*, p. 82.

9. This poem is not to be confused with the poem of the same title that appeared in *Great Praises*.

10. Journal entry for June 21, 1838, given in William M. Gibson and George Arms, eds., *Twelve American Writers* (New York, 1962), p. 49.

Chapter Five

1. See the bibliography in Roache, *op. cit.*

2. Donald Hall, Robert Pack, and Louis Simpson, eds., *The New Poets of England and America* (New York, 1957).

3. Donald M. Allen, ed., *The New American Poetry 1945-1960* (New York, 1960).

4. Ralph Mills, Jr., *Richard Eberhart* (Minneapolis, 1966).

5. *Ibid.*, p. 44.

6. M. L. Rosenthal, *The Modern Poets* (New York, 1960).

7. Cited in Note 7 to Chapter 2, above.

8. Stephen Stepanchev, *American Poetry Since 1945* (New York, 1965), pp. 8-11.

9. Peter L. Thorslev, Jr., "The Poetry of Richard Eberhart," in Edward Hungerford, ed., *Poets in Progress* (Chicago, 1957), p. 91.

10. In Allen, *op. cit.*, pp. 69-72; also in correspondence with me, especially in a letter dated October 12, 1966.

11. Letter to me, October 12, 1966.

Selected Bibliography

There is no complete bibliography of writing by and about Eberhart. Joel Roache's dissertation, cited below, gives a fairly comprehensive but still incomplete listing. Roache draws on unpublished sources in the Baker Library at Dartmouth College. The following selection not only makes use of these guides but also includes suggestions made by Eberhart himself.

PRIMARY SOURCES

1. Poetry

A Bravery of Earth. New York: Jonathan Cape and Harrison Smith, 1930.
Reading the Spirit. New York: Oxford University Press, 1937.
Song and Idea. New York: Oxford University Press, 1942.
Poems, New and Selected. Norfolk, Connecticut: New Directions, 1945.
Burr Oaks. New York: Oxford University Press, 1947.
Brotherhood of Man. Pawlet, Vermont: Banyan Press, 1949.
An Herb Basket. Cummington, Massachusetts: Cummington Press, 1950.
Selected Poems. New York: Oxford University Press, 1951.
Undercliff: Poems 1946-1953. New York: Oxford University Press, 1953.
Great Praises. New York: Oxford University Press, 1957.
Collected Poems 1930-1960. New York: Oxford University Press, 1960.
Collected Verse Plays. Chapel Hill: The University of North Carolina Press, 1962.
The Quarry. New York: Oxford University Press, 1964.
Selected Poems 1930-1965. New York: New Directions, 1965.
Thirty One Sonnets. New York: Eakins Press, 1967.
Shifts of Being. New York: Oxford University Press, 1968.

2. Prose

Biographical entry in Stanley Kunitz, ed., *Twentieth Century Authors.* First Supplement. New York, 1955.
"A Book About Modern Poetry." *Poetry,* LXXXII (August, 1953), 282-87.
"Deep, Lyrical Feelings," *New York Times Book Review,* CI (December 16, 1951), 4. Review of Theodore Roethke, *Praise to the End.*

171

"The Expense of Critical Reason." *Accent,* II (Autumn, 1941), 51-55.
Review of R. P. Blackmur, *The Expense of Greatness;* John Crowe
Ransom, *The New Criticism;* and Allen Tate, *Reason in Madness.*
"How I Write Poetry." Howard Nemerov, ed. *Poets on Poetry.* New
York, 1966.
"Major Poet and Literary Innovator." *New York Times Book Review,* C
(December 17, 1950), 1. Review of W. C. Williams, *The Col-
lected Later Poems.*
"Notes on Poetry." John Ciardi, ed. *Mid-Century American Poets.*
New York, 1950.
"On Theodore Roethke's Poetry." *Southern Review,* I (Summer, 1965),
612-20.
"Pound's New Cantos." *Quarterly Review of Literature,* V (1947),
174-91.
Proceedings, National Poetry Festival. Washington, D.C., 1962. Re-
marks by Eberhart, and some of his poems, are printed on
pp. 198-204, 287-88, and 343-46.
"Richard Eberhart Discusses Group of Young Poets on West Coast."
New York Times Book Review, VII (September 2, 1956), 1, 4.
"Robert Frost: His Personality." *Southern Review,* 2 (Autumn, 1966),
762-88.
"Tragedy as Limitation: Comedy as Control and Resolution." *Tulane
Drama Review,* VI (Summer, 1962), 3-14.
"A Vision of Life and Man that Drives the Poet On." *New York
Times Book Review,* CVII (September 14, 1958). Review of
W. C. Williams, *Paterson V.*
"Why I Say It in Verse." Paul A. Jorgensen and Frederick B. Shroyer,
eds. *A College Treasury* III. New York, 1956.
"Will and Psyche in Poetry." Don Cameron Allen, ed. *The Moment
of Poetry.* Baltimore, 1962.

SECONDARY SOURCES

ALVAREZ, ALFRED. *The Stewards of Excellence.* New York: Charles
Scribner's Sons, 1958. Says that Eberhart's "isolation" from any
philosophical system outside himself produces awkwardness in
writing. Eberhart and Robert Lowell, "the two most impressive
American poets since . . . the 'twenties," have in common only
this "powerful, shut-in awkwardness."
BEWLEY, MARIUS. Review of *Selected Poems. New York Review of
Books,* V (March 31, 1966), 20. Cites Eberhart as one who has
"rightly occupied an important and honorable place" but finds
his accomplishment "oddly inconclusive" and gives examples of
what he regards as posturing and bad rhetoric.
BLACKMUR, R. P. "Reading the Spirit." *Partisan Review,* V (February,
1938), 52-56. Says that the poetry is too rough, but that what
matters is that it gives off a great number of images and insights,
that in it "the rich material of everyman's dilemma is exposed."

BOOTH, PHILIP. "The Varieties of Poetic Experience." *Shenandoah,* XV (Summer, 1964), 62-69. Reviewing *The Quarry,* Booth remarks on the poet's "seeming innocence" and his independence from poetic fashions. Styles Eberhart a "religious romantic" whose intention is "to propose moral possibilities in a universe so complex that even its grandeur is all but incomprehensible."

CARRUTH, HAYDEN. "Errors of Excellence." *Nation,* CXCII (January 21, 1961), 63-64. A dozen of Eberhart's poems are "the equal of anything ever produced in America." Similarities to Auden, Dylan Thomas, and Stevens suggest that, despite his independence, Eberhart is using what is really the "central or common poetic style" of this century.

CIARDI, JOHN. "How Does a Poem Mean?" Herbert Barrows *et al,* eds. *An Introduction to Literature.* Boston: Houghton Mifflin Co., 1959. Uses Eberhart's "The Fury of Aerial Bombardment" to illustrate discussions of metrics and of poetic structure.

DICKEY, JAMES. "In the Presence of Anthologies." *Sewanee Review,* LXVI (1958), 309-10. Interesting as the opinion of an important contemporary poet, this brief notice of *Great Praises* finds the diction often turgid but values Eberhart's inspiration.

DONOGHUE, DENIS. "An Interview with Richard Eberhart." *Shenandoah,* XV (Summer, 1964), 5-29. The interviewer elicits from Eberhart several statements on the relationship between poetic inspiration and the world of affairs. He also questions Eberhart on the work of Williams, Eliot, and Stevens; on Christianity; and on the intentions of several poems.

―――――. "Richard Eberhart: *The Visionary Farms.*" *The Third Voice.* Princeton, N.J.: Princeton University Press, 1959. Though it finds the play a thesis drama with no real claim to originality, it discusses respectfully its use of "distortion and simplification" as semi-expressionist devices.

ENGEL, BERNARD F. "On the Accomplishment of Richard Eberhart." *South Florida Poetry Journal* (1970), 112-14. Remarks on Eberhart's mixture of the observed and the sensed to achieve unity.

―――――, ed. *The Achievement of Richard Eberhart.* Glenview, Illinois: Scott, Foresman and Co., 1968. Illustrates Eberhart's achievement in producing fine poetry that is aware of the claims of both the flesh and the spirit.

FEIN, RICHARD J. "The Cultivation of Paradox: The War Poetry of Richard Eberhart." *Forum,* X (Spring, 1969), 56-64. Uses several of Eberhart's poems on World War II themes to illustrate the assertion that in his poetry "the seemingly contradictory but exciting relationship between aggression and art, between war and aesthetics, advances a sense of the spiritual mystery of man." Praises the poet's creation of an "effective tension" which has its origin in "a beautiful unsureness."

GARRIGUE, JEAN. Review of *Shifts of Being.* *New York Times Book Review,* CXIX (January 12, 1969), 18. Terming Eberhart "one

of the best and most original poets of our time," Garrigue points
to a "double sense of the ironies" which he finds "more and more
essential to his tragic vision."

HALL, DONALD. "Method in Poetic Composition." *Paris Review,* I
(Autumn, 1953), 113-19. Contrasts Eberhart, seen as one be-
lieving that poetry arises from a divine madness, with Richard
Wilbur, seen as one believing in careful planning.

HOFFMANN, DANIEL. "Hunting a Master Image: The Poetry of Richard
Eberhart." *The Hollins Critic,* I (October, 1964), 1-12. Discusses
Eberhart's motives and individuality; concludes that "it seems
likely that a score or more of his poems will prove indestructible."

MARSHALL, JEFFREY. "An Interview with Richard Eberhart." *The
William and Mary Review,* II (Winter, 1964), 1-12. Questions
the poet about his relativism, various influences on him, verse
drama, the state of poetry, and several individual poems.

MARTZ, LOUIS. "The Virtues of Collection." *Yale Review,* L (March,
1961), 443-45. Calls "The Fury of Aerial Bombardment" a
classic and finds "broadening areas of experiment" in "The
Supreme Authority of the Imagination" and "The Hard Structure
of the World."

MILLS, RALPH J., JR. "Richard Eberhart." *Contemporary American
Poetry.* New York: Random House, 1965. Finds that Eberhart
has achieved a unity of view despite his recognition that "the
answers and lessons" in his art sometimes oppose each other.

————. *Richard Eberhart.* Minneapolis: University of Minnesota
Press, 1964. Number 55 in the University of Minnesota Pam-
phlets series. Places Eberhart with Stanley Kunitz and Theodore
Roethke as among leaders of the post-modern generation; says
that Eberhart's avoidance of movements has given him an
"independent availability to experience" which has enabled him
to accept both "the events of existence in the world" and "the
revelations of the spirit."

MONROE, HARRIET. "Brave Youth." *Poetry,* XXXVI (September, 1930),
343-44. Finds "rich growths here and there, and . . . rank patches
of weeds"; hopes that "Mr. Eberhart will succeed in disciplining
his muse without beating the life out of her."

ROACHE, JOEL H. III. "Never Blown Down in the Secret Heart."
South Florida Poetry Journal (1970), 108-11. Remarks on the
"spiritual persistence" that Eberhart exhibits in the face of
challenges from physical nature, illustrating this especially by
examining the poems "The Secret Heart" and "A Man Who Was
Blown Down by the Wind."

————. *Richard Eberhart: A Poet in America 1904-1961.* University
of Pennsylvania Ph.D. dissertation, 1967. Available as University
Microfilm No. 68-4611. Sees a move from early alienation to
later acceptance of American society; much valuable information
on the poet's career, most of it obtained through interviews and
close association with the poet.

SIMPSON, LOUIS. "Poets in Isolation." *Hudson Review,* X (Autumn, 1967), 458-59. Finds Eberhart's writing to be awkward and inchoate at times, yet sometimes able to "astonish us with a real grandeur of images."

THORSLEV, PETER L., JR. "The Poetry of Richard Eberhart." Edward B. Hungerford, ed. *Poets in Progress.* Chicago: Northwestern University Press, 1967. Concludes that Eberhart has some of the virtues of both academic poets and anti-intellectuals, "a keen intelligence, but also a warm humanity and a genuine inspiration."

VANAKOS, BYRON. "Eberhart: A Negative Report." *Poetry,* LXXXV (November, 1954), 106-8. Review of *Undercliff.* Though he praises the "many virtues" of earlier work, Vanakos finds here too much of the "primitive," a "dissociation from the responsibilities of content and form."

WRIGHT, JAMES. "Personal Testament." *New York Times Book Review,* CXVII (October 8, 1967), 20 and 22. Remarks that some passages in Eberhart's works are so rough-hewn that they drive his friends to despair, but says that some of his poems are a permanent part of the language. Finds the sonnets themselves undistinguished.

Index

(Articles such as "The" and "A" have not been considered in alphabetizing the Index.)